The Joys of Baking is a sweet meditation on why we bake,
on how what we make with our hands changes us, soothes, comforts,
and inspires us. Sam's generously personal stories and the collection
of recipes she braids into them encourage us to bake, to pay
attention as we stir and knead, and to reap each of the many
pleasures she describes. The book is a delight.

—DORIE GREENSPAN,
award-winning author of *Everyday Dorie* and *Dorie's Cookies*

◆ ◆ ◆

The Joys of Baking bursts with ripe fruits and berries,
dark, bittersweet chocolate, buttery tarts, whole grains, and
creamy custards—in short, all of my favorite things to bake . . . and eat!
Sprinkled with personal stories, Samantha Seneviratne's
gorgeously photographed cookbook will fill anyone's sweet spot.

—DAVID LEBOVITZ,
author of *My Paris Kitchen* and *The Perfect Scoop*

THE JOYS OF BAKING

THE JOYS OF BAKING

RECIPES AND STORIES
FOR A SWEET LIFE

Samantha Seneviratne

Riverhead Free Library
330 Court Street
Riverhead NY 11901

Running Press
PHILADELPHIA

Running Press
Hachette Book Group
1290 Avenue of the Americas, New York, NY 10104
www.runningpress.com
@Running_Press

Printed in China

First Edition: October 2019

Published by Running Press, an imprint of Perseus Books,
LLC, a subsidiary of Hachette Book Group, Inc.
The Running Press name and logo is a trademark of the
Hachette Book Group.

The Hachette Speakers Bureau provides a wide range
of authors for speaking events. To find out more, go to
www.hachettespeakersbureau.com or call (866) 376-6591.

The publisher is not responsible for websites
(or their content) that are not owned by the publisher.

Photographs copyright © 2019 by Julia Gartland
Print book cover and interior design by Amanda Richmond
Prop styling by Ali Slagle

Library of Congress Control Number: 2019940541

ISBNs: 978-0-7624-9253-4 (hardcover),
978-0-7624-9252-7 (ebook)

1010

10 9 8 7 6 5 4 3 2 1

For Artie: the sweetest bun of all

CONTENTS

INTRODUCTION

Several years ago, at the worst possible time, my dresser began to fall apart.

The drawers groaned complaints when I pulled at them. Splinters pricked my palms as I grabbed for socks in the middle of the night. The handle of the bottom drawer had come off altogether, so I just left it open, and the legs of my jeans were always trying to sneak out to party on their own. Even though it had seen better days, I didn't want to let it go.

I didn't want to let it go *because* it had seen better days. Fifteen years ago, the dresser was home to my brother's favorite red sweatshirt, his jeans, sweatpants, button-down shirts, and sweaters. It was dark, handsome, and substantial—the kind of thing a real grown-up would have in his apartment. I was envious. I remember visiting my brother in his tiny studio near Times Square. We would sit on the floor and lean against the dresser—practically his only furniture—while we ate his special mushroom pasta and talked about our plans.

When I inherited it, the dresser became an important landmark in my own life. Instead of filling it with our clothes, my husband, Augustine, thought to turn it into a makeshift hutch. Heavy cookware in the bottom, then stacks of plates, mismatched glassware, and cheap silverware, all the way up. We propped a faux-glitzy mirror on top and set out our alcohol. Not the bar at Balthazar, but nice. It was the beginning of our home together.

But those days were long over when I woke up one sunny summer morning and all of a sudden saw the dresser in a new light. My brother had died. My divorce was looming. Big pieces of veneer were flaking off, exposing the cheap wood underneath. Desperate to start over, I decided to get rid of it right away.

I had the good sense to take out all the drawers, but still the thing felt like an elephant's casket when I tried to budge it. Big and blocky, but also fragile somehow. It was completely unwilling to help me get on with my life. I think it was actually fighting me. I managed to slide it out the front door of my apartment and into the narrow hallway. I pushed and pulled and shimmied and got it to the edge of the first set of stairs. Six floors down to the curb, Fresh Kills Landfill, and a new start.

I decided to get under it. I would slide the beast down the stairs, guiding from the bottom. I thought my determination would overcome any weakness in my actual muscles.

I wrestled it down one flight, but then something shifted above me. The only thing I hadn't planned for was gravity. In one quick and heart-stopping motion, I was pinned against the rickety iron railing of my apartment building's stairway, five flights up.

The sharp wood corners dug into my forearms. The veins in my neck popped out against the strain. The old railing creaked. I thought about yelling for help, but I was still too full of pride. So, I stayed there, quivering and shaking from the strain and the fear, the dam holding back my panic and tears about to burst. No one was coming to help me. There was no one to call. No one was worrying about me. No one would know if I got hurt. Either this thing crushes me or I push back and get out from under—those were my choices.

Somehow, I managed the latter. I battled the thing back into my apartment, closed the door, and sat down on the floor, depleted, sad, and alone. For the better part of an hour I sat staring at the wall, surveying my situation. And then I stood up and reached for the blue and white bag of bread flour.

Cooking is a necessity. Everyone needs to eat. Preparing a special meal can be a joy, of course, but often it feels like a chore, just another item on an endless list of things that must get done.

Baking is different. Baking is a choice. Baking is never a necessity. No one needs a chocolate cake to survive. Except, sometimes, a chocolate cake is exactly what you need to survive. Sometimes, a chocolate cake is the only thing you need in the world. This is a book about and for those times.

Every baking project begins with the imagination of pleasure. Something sparks it. A desire: perfect plums at the market. A craving: salty-sweet. A memory: summer walks with ice cream. A feeling: the dizzy throes of new love. The project takes shape around an idea of sensuous experience. Sometimes, that means the physical satisfaction that comes from the act of creaming butter and sugar, folding pastry dough to create a lattice, or kneading bread. Other times, it means baking and eating and sharing and talking and laughing with a friend. Whatever the pleasure, however it originates and wherever it leads, baking is about making the pleasures you imagine real. Learning to bake is about learning to please yourself.

Yet in this age of Instagram, our baking lives have been hijacked by the hope of pleasing strangers. Seeking approval, we confine ourselves to one emotional register—picture-perfect and happy, exclamation point, exclamation point, exclamation point. Heart emoji, heart emoji, double-heart emoji.

My heart is not an emoji. Picture-perfect would be wonderful, but I also believe that a good, full, rich, and satisfying life contains wilder forms of joy.

The very first recipe in the first edition of *The Joy of Cooking* is not for an aspic, a consommé, or a cheese soufflé, as I would have guessed. It is not even cooking. It's a recipe for Gin Cocktail: Two parts gin, two parts orange juice, one part lemon juice, bitters.

The recipe speaks volumes, especially because Irma Rombauer published her book during the middle of Prohibition. Certainly a cocktail is a good way to start a meal. And it's definitely nice to have a fail-safe drink recipe at the ready for when dinner guests arrive early. But I suspect that in this case, Irma was the one who needed a drink.

Despite its title, Irma Rombauer's famous cookbook was born from catastrophe. Four months after the stock market crashed in October 1929, her husband killed himself. His death left her not only grieving but poor. Most of their savings had been in stocks, and she had no way to support herself. In the middle of those dire circumstances, Irma saw a need for a cookbook that took economic hard times into account, so she wrote *The Joy of Cooking* and published it herself with half of what was left of her meager savings. Her first edition, published in 1931, sold three thousand copies.

Since then, *The Joy of Cooking* has become one of the most popular and influential books in the world. It is authoritative, plucky, and reliable. What it is not is especially joyful—nor is it especially sad. The book's tragic backstory is nowhere to be found in its pages. According to her somewhat apologetic introduction to the first edition, Irma had no interest in making herself the story, or in writing about feelings, and she was embarrassed by and for those who did. But then, why talk of joy of at all? What exactly is the joy of, and in, cooking?

Perhaps Irma—writer and publisher both—simply made the book she thought she could sell, the book she thought the greatest number of people would like, the book she could use to feed her family. And given the circumstances, fair enough. Yet I can't help imagining the book that might have been. Irma's voice is winning. Her sense of humor comes through. She describes tongue in aspic as a "palatable dish." She defines *pot au feu* as "ice box soup." It's true that there is little uninhibited joy in *The Joy of Cooking*, but there is moxie. In Irma's writing, I hear a determined woman fighting back, seizing what chances she could. I see a real person, confronting emotionally complex circumstances, trying to cook her way through. To speak to the economic crisis of her day, Irma included plenty of recipes and tips for leftovers. But what about her recipes and tips for getting through a personal crisis? I bet they would have been pithy classics.

The Joys of Baking is inspired by the book that Irma Rombauer could have written. It's the story of baking my way through my own heartbreak—of what happened when the parts of my life I thought would be the best turned out to be the worst, and when the things I thought would make me happy almost wrecked me, and why they didn't. It's a book about joys, plural, about all the different sources and forms of joy that make up our real baking lives, the complexity of experiences and feelings that shape even our simplest baking projects. The sadness that gives way to strength. The wisdom that can come from loss. The vertigo of new love. The deep happiness of sharing delicious things with beloved people, the happiness so deep it sometimes feels like sadness. This is a book about how, when life gives you lemons, you make a Gin Cocktail, sing along with *Lemonade,* and put on a pot of curd. The recipes tell the stories of how I fell, how I rose, what I baked, and what it meant.

When I get up off the floor, I need a project that will be soothing, something that will feel good in my hands. One requiring just enough work to be rewarding, but no heavy lifting. Something I can sing to.

In my experience, singing and baking go hand in hand. As chief bread-bakers in our Oberlin co-op, my friend Amy and I spent many college afternoons making our special rosemary onion bread and switching between the lead roles from *Jesus Christ Superstar.* The whir and thump of the industrial Hobart mixer laid down the percussion for our spirited renditions of "I Don't Know How to Love Him." Where the lyrics said "Jesus," we subbed in the names of our latest love interests. The dank basement kitchen became our sanctuary and our stage. Every bake was another opportunity to rethink our harmonies, our dance moves, and our love lives. We baked and sang until we felt ready to face our not-so-complicated problems.

So, I decide to make bread. Flour is an all-purpose beginning, downy and fine and pure and light—the opposite of homicidal old furniture. I imagine a sweet loaf, enriched with extra eggs, butter, and sugar. Pillowy soft, subtly spiced, and gilded with a decadent swirl of chocolate.

I start with my favorite task. I bash green cardamom pods gently in my mortar, the eucalyptus buzz burning away my tears. I extract the tiny seeds, clean the mortar, and crush them again. They will go into the dough and become the soul of my bread. I find myself singing "I Dreamed a Dream" with earnest clarity, in true Anne Hathaway style. *Les Misérables* indeed.

I beat together a simple enriched dough. It starts sticky, unkempt, and lumpy. But I talk to my dough, and we work it out together. I take ultimate comfort in the reliability of my ingredients. I know how to do this. I feel it changing in my hands.

I knead the dough and it comes together lusciously. Enriched with extra butter, sugar, and eggs, it turns extra-soft, springy, supple, and taut. By now, my small kitchen countertop is covered in spatters of milk, a dusting of flour, and a broken egg, but I don't mind. My neighbor's dog is yipping along with my fudged key changes. Do I sound worse to him than he does to me? When I'm baking, I can tell myself little lies I want to be true. Clumsiness is charming. I have a lovely voice.

I move the dough to a buttered bowl, cover it, and set it aside for the first rise. Usually the tropical climate in my studio apartment drives me nuts, but today it's just right, a cozy home where my dough baby can grow. While it rises, I melt together butter, sugar, and chocolate to swirl through the middle of the loaf.

When my dough is puffed and ready, I pat it out flat and paint on the chocolate spackle with an offset spatula. I can imagine what it would feel like if my chocolate were actually oil paint, thick and glossy, and I was capturing a turbulent sea, whorls of dark waves covering the surface of my canvas. I roll, cut, and braid the loaf, and set it in a pan for another rise. An hour later, the bread is ready for the oven.

While it bakes, my house smells friendly again. The chocolate, butter, sugar, and cardamom swirl in the air and calm my nerves. Fantine is dead. Eponine is dead. But I'm reaching for those high notes in "A Heart Full of Love." Not quite getting there, but really going for them. I peek through the oven window for evidence of my competence and am reassured.

I shove the dresser into a corner and forget about it for now. It will have to live with being on the way out for a while. The bread is done. I burn my tongue on the first steaming bite.

A FEW KITCHEN NOTES

BAKING TIMES: Baking times in recipes are a general guide, not an exact science. A number of changing factors determine the length of time something will take to cook. Ovens vary. Ingredients vary. Bakers vary. When determining a bake time, it's best to consider the visual cues noted in the recipe first and the suggested baking times second: Always set a timer for five minutes sooner than the recommended bake time to check in. Use all of your senses to determine whether something is done and never set it and forget it.

That goes for rising times as well. It's always better to watch your dough rather than the clock.

BUTTER: Using unsalted butter for baking gives the baker the ability to control the salt in the finished dish, which is why I call for it in my recipes. But if you only have salted butter, go ahead and use it! No need for an extra shopping trip. Simply reduce the amount of kosher salt in the recipe. Room-temperature butter should be soft enough that you can easily press your finger into it, leaving a clear thumbprint, but not so soft that it is wet and greasy. To speed up the softening process, cut your measured butter into pieces.

Creaming butter and sugar is a technique used to add loft to baked goods. As you beat them together, the sugar actually cuts tiny bubbles into the butter. Those bubbles then trap the gas released by leavener and give the final cake a nice, fine texture. Starting with butter at the proper temperature is the best way to achieve this. You'll know when it's properly creamed when the mixture is pale yellow in color (not white, which would indicate that the mixture is overcreamed), it has fluffy peaks, and the sugar is mostly dissolved.

To "cut" the butter into a flour mixture means to incorporate it only up to the point where the mixture has an irregular, coarse, sandy texture and with pieces of butter that range from the size of quinoa to the size of peas. Those pieces of butter will melt in the oven and create pockets of steam. This is how we get flakiness in pie pastry and tender scones. A pastry blender makes this job easy, but if you don't have one, you can use two knives. Start with a knife in either hand and then slice the butter in between the two knives, mimicking the action of a pair of scissors. Repeat this until you have the appropriate consistency.

CARAMEL: People will tell you a million and one ways to prevent crystallization when making caramel, from brushing water on the sides of the pot to adding lemon juice. I haven't found many of those things to be necessary. I think it comes down to these key factors: Firstly, use a good-quality, heavy pot. Even heat is important and a flimsy pot won't do you any favors. Second, don't stir the caramel. Stirring encourages crystallization. Let the mixture simmer away until you start to see it getting darker in spots then gently swirl the pan to make sure it browns evenly. Last, avoid organic sugar or any brown sugars when making caramel. White refined sugar is much more reliable.

If the sugar crystalizes before it browns, don't panic. Simply add a tablespoon or two of water and swirl it in. The crystals should melt and you can start the process over again.

CHOCOLATE: *Melting chocolate:* Chocolate can scorch easily if exposed to high temperatures, so melting it takes a bit of care. I think the microwave method is the simplest. Set the chocolate in a microwave-safe bowl and heat for 10- to 15-second bursts, stirring in between. You can also melt chocolate in a double boiler on the stovetop, but be sure to keep moisture at bay as even a few drops could make it seize. The water should not touch the bottom of the pot containing the chocolate.

Tempering chocolate: Tempering chocolate makes it shiny and snappy versus something softer and meltier that's better stored in the fridge. It isn't difficult to do, but it does take a bit of patience. Here is how I temper dark chocolate, should you want to give it a shot.

This is called the "seeding method." Start with at least 1 pound of chopped semisweet chocolate. Do not use chips. Place 12 ounces of the chocolate in a microwave-safe bowl and melt it in 5- to 25-second bursts, stirring occasionally, until it is melted and the temperature registers between 114° and 118°F on an instant-read thermometer. Try fewer seconds as the temperature starts getting close so that you don't overshoot the mark. Remove the bowl from the microwave and stir in the remaining 4 ounces of chocolate, a little bit at a time, stirring in between each addition until the temperature has come down to 88° to 89°F. After a bit of practice, you can actually see and feel the chocolate fall into temper. It takes on a slightly looser quality and becomes shinier.

Now you're ready to coat anything and everything in tempered chocolate! For starters, try the Peppermint Snow Patties (page 86), the Salted Chocolate-Covered Chocolate Caramels (page 52), or the Caramel Cookie Bars (page 137). If the temperature of the chocolate falls below 88°F, rewarm it. If it goes above 91°F, start the process over again. When you are all finished, save any remaining chocolate, well wrapped at room temperature, for another day.

CITRUS: Freshly grated citrus zest adds robust flavor to baked goods. A Microplane makes easy work of grating citrus. Remove only the colored portion of the skin. The white pith is bitter. Once you've removed the zest, wrap citrus in plastic wrap to store. Without its protective covering, the fruit tends to dry out very quickly and you don't want to lose the precious juice inside!

COCONUT: Some recipes call for sweetened coconut and some call for unsweetened coconut. Be sure to take note before shopping.

EGGS: All the recipes in this book were developed with large eggs. Save the jumbo eggs for the Sunday scramble. Eggs should be at room temperature to bake.

FLOUR: Different types of flour are not necessarily interchangeable. Cake flour is finer and has less protein than all-purpose flour, for example. Be sure to read each recipe carefully and note the kind(s) of flour it calls for.

Properly measured flour can be the difference between a dense, sad cake and light, happy one. I'm a big believer in the scoop-and-sweep method to measure flour. Use a big spoon to scoop the flour into the measuring cup, without packing it in, and then use a knife to level it off cleanly. For the most accurate measure, use measuring cups meant for dry ingredients, as opposed to those clear measuring cups meant for liquids. I know this sounds nitpicky, but I promise you that it matters.

HAZELNUTS: Hazelnuts have a bitter, papery skin that must be removed before eating. It's easy to do. Simply toast the hazelnuts on a dry baking sheet at 350°F until the skins have started to crack and separate from the nut, about 10 minutes. Transfer the warm nuts to a clean dish towel, wrap them up, and rub them around. As they rub against one another, the skins will come off. Repeat the entire process, if necessary. But don't worry about getting every speck of skin. That could drive you nuts! Aim for about 75 percent clean. Let the nuts cool completely before proceeding with the recipe.

INSTANT ESPRESSO POWDER: Instant espresso powder is an intense form of instant coffee that dissolves easily in water. It makes a terrible espresso but adds wonderful depth to chocolate desserts. Look for it near the instant coffee in the supermarket or online. If you can't find instant espresso, you can use about double the amount of instant coffee.

LYLE'S GOLDEN SYRUP: Lyle's is a thick syrup made from sugarcane. I use it in my recipes where corn syrup would normally appear because it tastes excellent! My parents used to bring it back from trips to England when I was little, but it's much easier to find in the United States now. Look for it near the maple syrup and honey in your local supermarket, or in the British area of the international foods aisle.

PREPARING PANS: Buttering and flouring a baking pan ensures that your lovely cakes release like a dream. To do this properly, first butter the pan well. I like to use a pastry brush and softened butter to evenly coat the pan. Next, add a generous amount of flour to the pan and swirl it around to coat the pan evenly on both the bottom and sides of the pan. Now, flip the pan over and forcefully slam it against your work surface. Work out some of your aggressions. It feels great. The goal is to knock out all the excess flour. Your pan should look like your windshield after the very lightest dusting of snow.

SALT: I use Diamond Crystal kosher salt for my cooking and baking. If you are using Morton's kosher salt or table salt, you will want to take the salt down.

SPELT: You may have noticed that I use spelt flour quite a bit. While working on Martha Stewart's book *A New Way to Bake*, I fell in love with the ancient wheat's unique sweet, nutty flavor. I find that it adds a little something extra without the bitterness that can accompany other whole-grain flours. All-purpose flour makes a fine substitute for the days when you're feeling a little less adventurous.

SPICES: Spices contain aromatic oils that begin fade as soon they are ground. For the best flavor, experts will tell you to grind spices fresh every time you use them. I find the difference most pronounced in nutmeg and cardamom. For those two spices, I always call for "freshly ground" in my baking recipes. For ease (and sanity) I think that preground spices are just fine for the rest.

VANILLA: Fresh vanilla beans are a treat to bake with, but they can be pricy. I buy them in bulk online for much less than they are at the supermarket. Stored well wrapped in the freezer, they will last for years. But, if you don't have any beans handy, a tablespoon of pure vanilla extract is a decent swap for the seeds of one fresh bean.

CHAPTER ONE

COURAGE

Roller-skating

The sweet smell of imitation butter melting over freshly popped popcorn swirled in the air with the slightly dank reek of the old, red, hard-worn carpet. Stacy Q's "Two of Hearts" bumped through the sound system on Repeat. It was just the beat I needed to lace up in my roller skates and get out there.

Every Wednesday after school during second grade, I went roller-skating. The rink was one of the only places where I was fearless. For my first few minutes in skates, I always marveled at being so tall. Four wheels added about 3 inches to my height—a confidence boost right from the start. Clanging from the carpet to the shiny wooden floor, I prepared to fling myself into the circling pack. You had to choose a moment when there was just the right opening and go for it without hesitation. Then, lap after lap after cool lap. Taking turns by stretching one leg out to the side because I couldn't cross my skates over one another. I couldn't skate backward, either. I couldn't spin. But I was sturdy and strong. Sometimes my friend Jenny and I would hold hands and cruise for a song or two, but she couldn't keep up for more that. I could skate forever.

When I knew the words to the song, it was even better. Papa don't preach. I'm in trouble deep. And I could sing and dance and keep my balance just fine. Weightless with the wind in my bowl cut. Stale indoor breeze on my face. I felt as though I was flying. I was never afraid of falling. I knew I wouldn't. I was cool in the skating rink, if nowhere else. And I reveled in it.

After thirty minutes or so, it was time for a snack. My braking technique was a quick slam into one of the side walls, grabbing the bar just before irreparable skeletal damage was done, and then I'd glide onto the carpet, where the friction did its job. At the snack bar, infinite junk-food choices were illuminated in rotating cases and shiny displays. Slick, juicy hot dogs, heaped with chili or cheese, glowing pink cotton candy, ice-cream bars of all shapes and sizes. Two dollars could buy enough calories to sustain a small town. I always went right for the snow cones.

Jewel-like shaved ice sparkled in its paper cone. The vendor asked me which flavor I'd like as he pointed to the bottles of sugar syrup. Blood red, electric blue, neon green, traffic cone orange. These were not colors found in nature. But to me, they were beyond gorgeous. "Orange, please!" and he went to work, dousing the ice. Within seconds, it would melt into a saccharine mess without any distinguishable fruit flavor, but I couldn't resist. Stained-tongue bliss.

Because he knew how much I liked it, my father tried to re-create the fun of the skating rink at home. The glossy-smooth cement floors of our basement made the perfect track. He cleared a path so that I could fly through the three rooms in a circular motion, never stopping, loop after loop.

The only trouble was that I found the basement to be a terrifying place. Boxes piled high hid ghosts and trolls. Invisible spiderwebs brushed my face everywhere. Pipes burped and floorboards creaked. The whole thing was saturated with the damp, dark earth smell of a tomb—far worse than the town rink.

But if I flicked on the light at the top of the stairs, I could get to the bottom fast, put on my skates, and become invincible. I zipped from one room to the other, tapping the metal chains that hung from the naked lightbulbs as I passed. I never would have done it on foot. Too slow and too scary! But on wheels, I flew. At first I was careful not to look into any of the corners, for fear of what might be lurking there. I never stayed still in one place. But after a few laps I could let my guard down. And that feeling of lightness came back.

I haven't laced up a pair of roller skates in decades, but the smoothness under my feet, a sugar high, and a syrup-stained tongue still mean pure childhood bliss to me. Today, I made a cool and slippery sherbet flavored with the most electric-colored fruit I could find. Blood orange juice and ginger, reminiscent of those perfect snow cones, but with more oomph. These days it takes a bit more flavor to be fearless.

Blood Orange and Ginger Sherbet

MAKES ABOUT 1 QUART SHERBET

Blood oranges are grown all over the Mediterranean and in parts of the United States, but I like to use the Sicilian variety—more for the image they inspires than the taste. The volcanic soil, hot days, and cold nights around Mount Etna in Sicily make the fruit itself a sweet, juicy volcano.

½ cup Lyle's Golden Syrup

½ cup granulated sugar

1 (2-inch) piece fresh ginger, peeled and thinly sliced (about ¼ cup)

2 cups blood orange juice (from about 13 oranges)

2 tablespoons freshly squeezed lemon juice

1¼ cups heavy cream

Pinch of kosher salt

Set a loaf pan in the freezer.

In a small saucepan, bring the golden syrup, sugar, and ginger, plus ⅓ cup of water, to a simmer over medium heat. Continue to cook, stirring often, until the mixture has thickened slightly, about 5 minutes. Remove from the heat and let cool.

In a large bowl, combine the orange and lemon juice, cream, salt, and cooled syrup mixture. Chill until very cold.

Strain the mixture through a fine-mesh sieve, then freeze the mixture in an ice-cream maker according to the manufacturer's instructions. Transfer the sherbet to the prepared pan, cover with plastic wrap, and freeze completely, at least 12 hours. Let the sherbet stand at room temperature for a few minutes to temper before serving.

MOM

I found an old picture of my mother in a box of photos at my grandmother's house in Sri Lanka. It had the orange patina of a photograph from the past. She has long hair tied into a low ponytail, a signature style of her youth that I never witnessed in person. She's seated at a wooden table, cutting what looks like an apple. There are small bags and bowls of food around her. The caption scrawled on the back in blue pen told of preparing a meal in the new house.

It was one of the photos she had sent back to her mother after she and my dad had moved to the States in 1969. It's clearly a posed shot. Nothing about what she's doing looks like an effective way to prepare a meal. She's seated. Her knife is too small. She has a funny smile on her face. She was only nineteen. When I look at that picture, I see the sweet gesture. Mom and Dad didn't want their parents to worry about them all alone in a new country. So, they set up a picture that would look like abundance, comfort, and competence, to set everyone at ease back home.

I think often about my parents' first years in America. They moved from tropical Sri Lanka to snowbound Manchester, Connecticut. My dad was doing his internship at Manchester Memorial Hospital while Mom spent her days at home, slightly afraid to leave the modest apartment they rented above a busy doctor's office.

Everything was different about her new home. The air was drier. The trees were tidier and less lush. The streets were paved clean and devoid of elephants. Even the way the sun shone in the sky seemed bluer and less orange. In Sri Lanka, her airy hilltop house was never empty. In addition to her parents and her sister, there was an endless stream of visitors—rivers of aunties and uncles and cousins that never ran dry, bringing with them sweets for tea, local gossip, and lots of giggling. I bet the unfamiliar quiet of Manchester hurt after a while.

But she managed. My mom and dad managed together. They settled in a new country, with new customs and new foods. They set up photo shoots to prove that they were home until Connecticut really felt like home. Two years later, they had my brother. By then, the pictures of her holding her son reveal a different gal altogether. She's facing the camera. No sheepish grin. She's wearing a supershort dress, beehive hairdo, and go-go boots. She looks beautiful, confident, and happy. She looks courageous. When I look at those pictures, I feel proud.

The other day, out of nowhere, my mother called me to ask me how to get a better texture on her pound cake. Hers had come out a bit dense. My mom would be the first person to tell you that she's not a baker. She just never has been interested in the precision and patience it requires. I was surprised she had attempted a pound cake at all. Assuming she had found a recipe online, but intrigued and touched by her interest in making the perfect pound cake, I asked her the usual questions: Did you cream the butter and sugar for long enough? Is your baking powder old? How many eggs does the recipe have you use? As we dug deeper, it became clear that she wasn't using a recipe at all. "Well, I just combined one cup of flour, two sticks of butter, and three eggs." She had improvised a pound cake, and called to ask me why it didn't come out right. She wasn't far off from the classic pound cake ratio, but she didn't know the most crucial fact. As the name implies, it's the weight of each ingredient that must be equal when making a pound cake.

My mom's gaff made me laugh. Over the years I've talked to so many people who find baking intimidating. Those who avoid the extra measuring and care that it takes like the plague. Not my mom. She simply dives in with utter fearlessness. She doesn't know what she doesn't know and doesn't care.

Fake it until you make it. It's one of the most overused adages, but it's the most useful. As a cookbook author, I'm not going to encourage people to attempt cakes without recipes on a daily basis. But I have learned something about baking from my beautiful mom. Fearlessness is delicious. Bake courageously, my loves.

Coconut and Passion Fruit Pound Cake

MAKES 1 LOAF

This one is for my mom. It's a simple pound cake inspired by the flavors of her tropical home. True pound cake relies on the lift that comes from creaming the butter and sugar perfectly. This recipe includes a little bit of insurance in the form of baking powder. It's a great beginner cake. Easy to make yet special.

In most recipes, I call for unsweetened shredded coconut, but this loaf is an exception. The sugar and moisture that comes from classic sweetened shredded coconut is important for the soft texture of this cake.

Preheat the oven to 350°F. Butter and flour an 8½ x 4½-inch loaf pan.

In a large bowl, whisk together the flour, baking powder, and salt. In a 2-cup measuring cup, whisk together the buttermilk and the passion fruit pulp and seeds.

With an electric mixer on medium speed, beat the butter, sugar, and coconut oil in a large bowl until pale and fluffy, about 3 minutes. Add the eggs, 1 at a time, scraping down the sides of the bowl occasionally.

Alternate adding the flour mixture and the buttermilk mixture to the egg mixture, starting and ending with the flour mixture. Stir in 1 cup of the toasted coconut.

Transfer the batter to the prepared pan and smooth the top. Sprinkle the top with the remaining ¼ cup of coconut. Bake until a toothpick inserted into the center comes out clean, 60 to 70 minutes. Transfer the pan to a wire rack to cool for 1 hour, then remove the cake from the pan and let cool completely.

½ cup/1 stick unsalted butter, at room temperature, plus more for pan

2 cups all-purpose flour, plus more for pan

2 teaspoons baking powder

½ teaspoon kosher salt

1 cup buttermilk, at room temperature

¼ cup passion fruit pulp and seeds (from 4 to 5 fruit)

1 cup granulated sugar

¼ cup melted virgin coconut oil

3 large eggs, at room temperature

1¼ cups sweetened flaked coconut, toasted, divided

Banana Date Bread with Lime

MAKES 1 LOAF

I was four years old when we moved into a brand-new house in South Windsor, Connecticut. One afternoon, my father decided I needed friends and walked me and Norman down to the local playground to meet the neighborhood children. Norman gave me strength. A sweet, fuzzy-headed, thumb-sucking baby monkey doll. To rest, he slipped perfectly inside an 8-inch yellow felt banana-shaped sleeping bag. Norman was my comfort and conversation starter when I met new kids. I can't decide whether I've heard the playground story so many times that I think I remember it, or if I actually do. But the vision of us is seared in my mind. My dear dad and me, hand in hand, me clutching Norman and his banana for dear life, silently walking down the street, both a little fearful about the next steps.

Back then, Norman and his banana were my ice-breakers. Now, it's the banana bread I offer up as I walk into the new and unfamiliar. Neither has ever let me down.

6 tablespoons/¾ stick unsalted butter, at room temperature, plus more for pans

1½ cups all-purpose flour, plus more for dusting

1 teaspoon baking powder

1 teaspoon kosher salt

½ teaspoon baking soda

⅔ cup granulated sugar

4 teaspoons finely grated lime zest (from 3 limes)

2 large eggs, at room temperature

1¼ cups mashed banana (from about 2 large bananas)

2 teaspoons pure vanilla extract

6 ounces pitted dates, finely chopped (1 cup)

Preheat the oven to 350°F. Butter and flour an 8½ x 4½-inch loaf pan.

In a medium bowl, whisk together the flour, baking powder, salt, and baking soda and set aside. With an electric mixer on medium speed, beat the butter, sugar, and lime zest in a large bowl until light and fluffy, about 3 minutes. Beat in the eggs, 1 at a time, scraping down the sides of the bowl as necessary. Beat in the banana and vanilla and fold in the dates. Fold the dry ingredients into the wet ingredients.

Transfer the batter into the prepared pan and bake until a skewer inserted into the center comes out with moist crumbs attached, 55 to 65 minutes. Transfer the pan to a wire rack to cool for 15 minutes, then flip the loaf out of the pan, turn it right-side up, and let it cool completely.

Store leftovers in an airtight container at room temperature for up to 3 days or frozen for up to 1 month.

Chocolate Cardamom Babka

MAKES 1 LOAF

I have developed my own way of testing bread dough to make sure it will bake up beautifully. I call it the pudge test. Once you've kneaded your dough until it's smooth and ready to rise, give it a little squeeze and a kiss. If it feels like a chubby baby thigh, you've done it exactly right. It should give, but just a little. Soft and squishy, but still holding its shape. Bravo! Aim for pudgy babies, in baking as in mothering.

If kissing your dough feels more like kissing your lovely grandmother's cheek, you probably need to add a little bit more flour. Slack, overly wet dough doesn't rise properly and can spread out instead of up. And if your dough feels like what I would imagine Jennifer Aniston's thigh feels like, you need to add a little more liquid. Tight and taut looks good on her, but will lead to a dry bread. Got it?

My vote is always for freshly ground cardamom. It's much tastier than the preground stuff. The extra minute of work will pay off. I promise.

Prepare the dough: Bring the milk just to a boil in a small pot over medium heat. Watch closely to ensure that the milk doesn't boil over. Transfer the milk to a liquid measuring cup and top it off with enough water to bring the level back to ½ cup. Let cool to 105° to 110°F. (It should be warm to the touch but not too hot.) Stir in the yeast and 1 teaspoon of the sugar and let stand until foamy, about 5 minutes. Add the egg and stir to combine.

In a the bowl of a stand mixer fitted with the paddle attachment, or in a large bowl and using a wooden spoon, combine the remaining ¼ cup of sugar and the bread flour, cardamom, and salt on low speed. Add the milk mixture and mix just until combined.

Switch to the dough hook and knead the dough on low speed, about 3 minutes. Alternatively, knead the dough by hand in the bowl until it comes together then tip it out onto a work surface and knead for about 6 minutes. Add the butter, a piece or two at a time. It may look as if it's not getting in there, but don't worry, it will; just keep adding and kneading. (You might have to stop the mixer and knead the butter in with your hands for a minute to get it started.) Once incorporated, increase speed to medium and knead the dough for another few minutes, or until it is smooth and elastic. If you are kneading by hand, you may want to use a dough scraper in one hand to help incorporate the butter. At this point you may add up to 2 more tablespoons of flour, if necessary, but do not add too much.

(continued on page 23)

DOUGH:

½ cup whole milk

1½ teaspoons active dry yeast

¼ cup plus 1 teaspoon granulated sugar, divided

1 large egg, at room temperature

2 cups bread flour, plus more as needed

1 teaspoon freshly ground cardamom, or ½ teaspoon preground

½ teaspoon kosher salt

4 tablespoons/½ stick unsalted butter, at room temperature, cut into ½-inch cubes, plus more for rising bowl and pan

Transfer the dough to a lightly buttered large bowl, fold it in on itself at 12, 3, 6, and 9 o'clock, flip it over, cover it with plastic wrap, and set aside in a warm, draft-free place to double in size. This could take 30 minutes or as long as 2 hours, depending on how warm your house is. It's best to just keep an eye on it and watch the dough rather than the clock.

Tip the dough out onto a work surface. Gently press out the air and fold the dough in on itself at 12, 3, 6, and 9 o'clock. Turn it over and pop it back in the buttered bowl for another rise. Butter an 8½ x 4½-inch loaf pan. Line it with parchment with a two-inch overhang on two sides.

Prepare the filling: Melt the butter over medium heat in a small saucepan. Remove the pan from the heat, add the chocolate, and let stand 1 minute. Stir until smooth. Then, stir in the sugar, cocoa powder, and salt. You should have a smooth paste. Let cool slightly.

Once the dough has almost doubled again, tip the dough onto a lightly floured work surface. Roll out the dough into a 16 x 10-inch rectangle. Spread the filling evenly over the surface. Starting with 1 of the short ends, roll up the dough and pinch to seal. Using a bench scraper or a sharp knife, cut the roll in half lengthwise. Turn the pieces so that cut side is facing up. Pinch the pieces together at 1 end, crisscross them tightly, and pinch them at the other end to seal. (Don't worry—this step is bound to be a little messy. Just do your best and it will be lovely.) Transfer the twist to the prepared loaf pan, cut sides up. Cover lightly with plastic wrap, and set aside to rise just to the edge of the loaf pan. This could take anywhere from 1 to 3 hours, depending on the temperature of the room.

Meanwhile, preheat the oven to 375°F. Bake the loaf until deep golden brown and the internal temperature has reached 190°F, 30 to 40 minutes.

Meanwhile. prepare the syrup: In a small saucepan, heat the sugar and ¼ cup of water over medium heat. Cook, stirring, until the sugar has dissolved. Set aside to cool.

Transfer the loaf in the pan to a wire rack. With a wooden skewer, poke holes all over the loaf. Pour the syrup over the warm loaf. Let the loaf cool for 20 minutes, then lift the loaf out of the pan to cool completely. Or gobble it up warm.

FILLING:

3 tablespoons unsalted butter

2¼ ounces semisweet chocolate, finely chopped (about ½ cup)

3 tablespoons granulated sugar

2 tablespoons Dutch-processed or natural cocoa powder

½ teaspoon kosher salt

SYRUP:

¼ cup granulated sugar

Coconut and Berry Cream Roll

SERVES 8 TO 10

Imagine a world where no one understands you. Everything is oversized and just out of reach. You can barely lift your own head. You spend so much time lying your back that you start to lose your hair in one very specific, 2-inch patch on the back of your noggin. The indignity. Then, one day you find the courage and the strength from deep within. That music box is just 1 inch too far to the right. Flex the core. Buck the legs. Strain the neck. Ooomph! The baby rolled over today and I have never been so proud. So, I baked a cake in his honor.

To toast coconut, spread it out on a dry, rimmed baking sheet and bake it for 8 to 10 minutes at 350°F. Set a timer and watch it closely. Burnt coconut is a real heartbreaker.

Coconut oil, for pan

1¾ cups shredded, unsweetened coconut, toasted, divided

1 cup all-purpose flour

¼ cup cornstarch

½ teaspoon coarse salt

6 large eggs, at room temperature, separated

½ plus ⅓ cup granulated sugar, divided

⅓ cup coconut milk

1 teaspoon pure vanilla extract

Confectioners' sugar for dusting

TO FINISH:

1 pound mixed fresh strawberries (sliced if large), raspberries, and blueberries (about 3 cups), plus more for serving

1 tablespoon granulated sugar

1½ cups cold heavy cream

1 tablespoon confectioners' sugar, plus more for dusting

Preheat the oven to 350°F. Oil a 17 x 12-inch rimmed baking sheet. Line with parchment and oil the parchment. Sprinkle the parchment evenly with 1¼ cups of the coconut.

In a medium bowl, whisk together the flour, cornstarch, salt, and the remaining ½ cup of coconut. In a large bowl, with an electric mixer on high speed, beat the egg yolks and ½ cup of the granulated sugar until opaque, about 1 minute. Add the coconut milk and vanilla on medium speed, then increase the speed to high and continue to beat until the mixture is pale yellow, fluffy, and about doubled in size, 6 to 8 minutes. Set aside.

With clean beaters, in a clean bowl, beat the egg whites on high speed until they have lost that yellow hue, about 1 minute. While beating, pour in the remaining ⅓ cup of sugar. Continue to beat until you have stiff, shiny peaks, 4 to 5 minutes.

With a large rubber spatula, fold the flour mixture into the egg yolk mixture. Then, carefully fold the egg white mixture into the egg yolk mixture, taking care not to deflate it. Dollop the batter onto the prepared pan and then use a long, offset spatula to spread it out evenly. Again, try not to deflate the batter too much. (Without leavener, the whipped eggs are what lift the cake.)

Bake the cake until light golden brown and set, 20 to 24 minutes. Meanwhile, set a clean dish towel on a work surface and sprinkle it evenly with confectioners' sugar. Gently press the center of the cake and it should spring back. Cut around the edges of the warm cake with a sharp knife to release it from the pan, then invert it onto the prepared dish towel. Remove the parchment paper. Roll up the towel and the cake, starting with the short end, and transfer it to a wire rack to cool completely.

To finish: Toss the berries with the granulated sugar and refrigerate until ready to serve, at least 1 hour. Whip the cream and tablespoon of confectioners' sugar to stiff peaks. (Do not overwhip.) Unroll the cake. Spread with the whipped cream and top evenly with the berries. Roll the cake back up and transfer to a serving plate. To serve, sprinkle the cake with confectioners' sugar and serve with extra berries.

Earl Grey Pain au Chocolat

MAKES 9 CROISSANTS

In 1988, I was nine years old. That was also the year the beautiful Irish songstress Enya came out with her ethereal hit "Sail Away." Even at nine, I knew it was a great song. Inspired by those early Calgon commercials (Remember? "Calgon, take me away.") I would swipe a couple of lavender-scented bath oil beads from my mother, run a deep tub, and luxuriate with Enya filling my ears and let the stress of my owl pellet dissection report just wash away. Those baths gave me the strength to take on another day of fourth grade. Nowadays, I turn to pastry for stress relief. Spending an afternoon focused on nothing but folding butter into a yeasty dough takes me away for a sweet while.

If Earl Grey isn't your cup of tea, feel free to omit the pastry cream. A simple pain au chocolat never hurt anyone.

DOUGH:

⅔ cup whole milk, warmed (110°F)

3 tablespoons granulated sugar, divided

1 tablespoon active dry yeast

1¾ cups all-purpose flour, plus more for rolling

1 cup/2 sticks cold unsalted butter, cut into ½-inch pieces (no smaller)

1 teaspoon kosher salt

EARL GREY CREAM:

1 cup whole milk

1 tablespoon loose Earl Grey tea

¼ cup granulated sugar

2 tablespoons cornstarch

3 large egg yolks

TO FINISH:

3⅜ ounces semisweet chocolate, chopped (¾ cup)

1 large egg, lightly beaten

Prepare the dough: In a small bowl, combine the milk and 2 teaspoons of the sugar. Stir in the yeast and let stand until foamy and cool, about 10 minutes. (You don't want the butter to melt in the next step.)

Meanwhile, toss together the flour, butter, salt, and remaining sugar in a separate large bowl. Add the milk mixture to the flour mixture and, using a rubber spatula, fold until evenly moistened. Take care not to incorporate the butter. You want those butter pieces to stay whole. Turn out the dough onto a piece of plastic wrap, shape into a small rectangle, and wrap well. Chill for at least 3 hours or up to 3 days.

On a lightly floured surface, let the dough warm up for a minute or two. (The butter should be about the same consistency as the dough. If the butter is too cold, it will break into pieces instead of rolling out evenly.) With a lightly floured rolling pin, roll the dough into a 10 x 16-inch rectangle, with the short side facing you. Fold the dough into thirds like a letter: the top third down and the bottom third up over middle. Use a bench scraper to help lift and fold the dough as necessary. At this point, the dough will be rough and shaggy with visible butter pieces. As you roll and fold the dough, it will come together. Flip the dough over and rotate it so the folded edge is to the left and the seam is down. Repeat this full process 2 more times, dusting the work surface, your hands, and the rolling pin with flour as necessary. Wrap the dough with plastic wrap and refrigerate for at least 30 minutes. Repeat the entire process once more for a grand total of 6 turns. If the dough starts to fight you and become difficult to work with at any point, just pop it into the fridge for an extra rest. Wrap the dough and refrigerate it for at least 6 hours, or overnight. (continued on page 28)

Prepare the Earl Grey cream: In a small saucepan, bring the milk to a boil over medium-high heat. (Keep a close eye on the pot as milk loves to boil over!) Remove the pot from the heat and add the tea leaves. Cover and let stand for at least 20 minutes.

Set a fine-mesh sieve over a small bowl. In a separate small bowl, whisk together the sugar and cornstarch. Slowly add about ¼ cup of the milk mixture to the sugar mixture, while whisking, to create a smooth paste. Whisk in the egg yolks until smooth. Add this mixture back to the warm milk and whisk until smooth. Return the pot to the heat and cook until the milk mixture is thick enough to coat the back of a spoon, about 2 minutes. Immediately strain the pastry cream through the sieve, stirring to help it through. Discard any solids left behind. Press a piece of plastic wrap into the surface of the pastry cream and chill until completely cold.

Line 2 rimmed baking sheets with parchment. On a lightly floured surface, roll the dough into an 11½ x 13½-inch rectangle. Using a sharp knife or a pastry cutter, cut the dough into 3 long sections lengthwise, then make 2 cuts across for a total of 9 equal rectangles. Working with 1 piece at a time, gently stretch the dough a bit to make the rectangle slightly longer. Brush the short edges of the rectangle with the egg wash. Spread about 2 tablespoons of pastry cream over the top of the dough rectangle. Next, sprinkle 4 teaspoons of chocolate in a line horizontally across the center. Then, fold the top over the chocolate and the bottom up and over the top to make a neat roll. Set the roll on the prepared pan, seam-side down. Cover with plastic and repeat with the remaining rectangles. (At this point, you could wrap the baking sheet well with plastic wrap and refrigerate overnight. The next day, about 2 hours before you'd like fresh croissants, take them out and continue with the rest of the recipe.)

Let the dough stand until puffed. Make sure to note the thickness of the dough when you first set it aside and use their growth as a guide. Sometimes I even take a quick picture. The croissants are ready to bake when the dough looks puffy and it bounces back slowly when pressed lightly. That's usually about 30 to 45 minutes, but it all depends on how the dough is and how warm your house is. While the dough is rising, preheat the oven to 425°F.

Gently brush each croissant with the egg wash. Bake 1 pan at a time until the pastry is golden brown and puffed, 10 to 15 minutes. Let cool slightly on the baking sheet. Repeat with the remaining pan. Serve warm.

Spicy Chocolate Hazelnut Biscotti

MAKES ABOUT 5 DOZEN BISCOTTI

Tummy ache. Headache. Heartache. Homesick. Take two slices of toast and call me in the morning.

A slice of bread, lightly toasted and liberally slathered with salty butter, takes the edge off all pains. Chewy, warm, uncomplicated but deeply delicious, I'd always like a slice of toast when I'm feeling blue. It's even better when administered by a loving friend along with a hug and a smile.

Biscotti are the toast of the cookie world. The dough is baked once in the form of a loaf, and then sliced and baked again until crisp. These chocolate biscotti are dotted with hazelnuts and chocolate chunks, and flavored with cinnamon and a bit of cayenne. Feel free to eat them long after breakfast is over.

Preheat the oven to 350°F.

In a small bowl, whisk together the flour, cocoa powder, baking powder, cinnamon, salt, and cayenne. In a large bowl, using an electric mixer, beat the granulated sugar and butter on medium speed until fluffy, about 3 minutes. Add the eggs, 1 at a time, and beat until combined. Add the flour mixture and beat until just combined. Beat in the hazelnuts and chocolate. The dough will be sticky.

On a lightly floured surface, split the dough in half. Roll each half into a 12-inch log. Transfer the 2 logs to a parchment-lined baking sheet, placing them at least 2 inches apart, and brush off any excess flour. Using your fingers, gently press the top of each log so it is about 2 inches wide. Brush the top of each log with the beaten egg white and sprinkle with sanding sugar. Bake until puffed and set, 25 to 29 minutes. The top will look dry and cracked. Transfer the baking sheet to a wire rack to cool completely. Lower the oven temperature to 325°F.

Transfer the logs to a cutting board. With a serrated knife, cut each log on the diagonal into ¼-inch slices. Transfer the slices to parchment-lined baking sheets and bake until the cookies are crisp, 10 to 15 minutes. Transfer the cookies to a wire rack to cool completely.

2 cups all-purpose flour, plus more for the surface

¾ cup cocoa powder, Dutch-processed or natural, sifted

2 teaspoons baking powder

1 teaspoon ground cinnamon

¾ teaspoon kosher salt

¼ to ½ teaspoon ground cayenne pepper

1¼ cups granulated sugar

6 tablespoons/¾ stick unsalted butter, at room temperature

3 large eggs, at room temperature

4½ ounces hazelnuts, toasted, skinned, and finely chopped (1 cup)

4½ ounces bittersweet chocolate, chopped (1 cup)

TO FINISH:

1 large egg white, lightly beaten

Sanding sugar for sprinkling

Apricot Frangipane Phyllo Tart

SERVES 12

When my son was about one year old, I applied to volunteer in the neonatal intensive care unit of my local hospital as an official baby cuddler. Research indicates that babies in the NICU do better when snuggled. Getting the job fulfilled the last of my childhood professional goals: cookie baker, book maker, and baby lover. The pinnacle.

To prepare for my interview, I needed to imagine how I want those babies to feel in my arms. Secure, loved, protected, warm, and brave enough to survive and thrive. The fruit in this tart is similar. It starts tense and firm, perhaps even a bit underripe. But once enveloped in buttery comfort of the toasted hazelnut frangipane and the warmth of the oven, they soften, relax, sweeten, and plump.

Prepare the crust: Preheat the oven to 350°F. Butter a 12 x 8-inch rectangular tart pan with a removable bottom. (Alternatively, you could use a 9-inch round tart pan with a removable bottom.) Set the phyllo on a work surface and cover with plastic wrap.

Working with 1 sheet at a time, butter 1 side of the phyllo with a pastry brush. Sprinkle with some of the granulated sugar and fold the sheet in half. Butter the top. Lay the sheet onto half of the prepared pan, butter-side up, with about ½ inch of the pastry hanging outside of the pan. Repeat with another sheet, butter, and sugar. Add the new sheet to the other side of the pan. Continue this process, buttering and sugaring the phyllo, folding it over, and laying it in the pan. The pieces can overlap every which way, but you want to eventually build up a crust that extends about ½ inch all the way around the pan. Fold and ruffle the edges however necessary to create an even border. Set the pan on a parchment-lined rimmed baking sheet and bake until light brown, 15 to 18 minutes.

Meanwhile, prepare the filling: In a food processor, combine 1 cup of the hazelnuts and the brown sugar, flour, and salt and process until very finely ground. Add the butter and ginger and process until smooth. Add the eggs and process until smooth. Coarsely chop the remaining ½ cup of hazelnuts and set aside.

Remove the crust from the oven and pour in the filling. Spread into an even layer and top with the fruit and chopped hazelnuts. Return the tart to the oven and bake until the filling is puffed, set, and golden brown around the fruit, 40 to 50 minutes. (If you used a round tart pan, it may take a few extra minutes to bake.) Serve warm or at room temperature. This tart is best the day it's made.

PHYLLO CRUST:

8 sheets phyllo, thawed if frozen

½ cup/1 stick unsalted butter, melted

¼ cup granulated sugar

FILLING:

6¾ ounces hazelnuts, toasted and skinned (1½ cups), divided

⅔ cup packed light brown sugar

1 tablespoon all-purpose flour

1 teaspoon kosher salt

4 tablespoons/½ stick unsalted butter, at room temperature

3 tablespoons finely chopped crystallized ginger

2 large eggs, at room temperature

12 ounces fruit, such as apricots and/or plums, pitted and sliced (2 cups)

Mascarpone Gingerbread Bars

SERVES 16

I sat outside my eight-week-old son's bedroom, clutching a plastic kitchen timer, staring at the seconds ticking away. Every wail made me wince. The timer was the only thing keeping my anxiety in check. Three minutes felt like 45. I had always planned to sleep-train my baby. I just didn't know how much it would hurt my heart.

I looked to the fridge for a way to keep my mind busy. I found mascarpone cheese—sweet and sultry, delightfully dense like cream cheese, with the fresh dairy shock of real cream. I imagined a sticky ginger cake to go with it, something soft and comforting, fragrant but not too sharp. I wanted the mascarpone to settle into its cake bedding, relaxed and happy, the two becoming one. And, of course, I needed something that could be made by hand. A mixer would only startle my little dreamer.

While the cake baked, he slept, and the ginger in the air soothed my frayed nerves.

GINGERBREAD BATTER:

2 cups all-purpose flour

1 tablespoon ground ginger

1½ teaspoons ground cinnamon

½ teaspoon baking soda

½ teaspoon kosher salt

¼ teaspoon freshly ground nutmeg

⅛ teaspoon ground cloves

¾ cup/1½ sticks unsalted butter, melted, plus more for pan

¾ cup packed dark brown sugar

½ cup granulated sugar

⅓ cup unsulfured molasses

2 large eggs, at room temperature

MASCARPONE BATTER:

1 large egg, at room temperature

1 cup mascarpone cheese, at room temperature

1 tablespoon granulated sugar

½ teaspoon pure vanilla extract

Prepare the gingerbread batter: Preheat the oven to 350°F. Butter a 9-inch square baking pan and line it with parchment, with a 2-inch overhang on 2 opposite sides.

In a small bowl, whisk together the flour, ginger, cinnamon, baking soda, salt, nutmeg, and cloves. In a large bowl, whisk together the melted butter, brown sugar, granulated sugar, and molasses, then whisk in the eggs. Add the flour mixture and fold to combine.

Prepare the mascarpone batter: In a small bowl, whisk the egg lightly. Add the mascarpone, granulated sugar, and vanilla.

Add the gingerbread batter and the mascarpone batter in alternating scoops to the prepared pan, then use a butter knife to swirl the 2 mixtures together. Bake until a knife inserted into the center comes out clean, 30 to 40 minutes. Transfer the pan to a wire rack to cool completely.

Using the parchment overhang as handles, transfer the cake to a cutting board. Cut into 16 squares.

Nectarine Galette with Sour Cherry Jam

SERVES 8

A fruit galette is the workhorse of the sweet kitchen. Freeing yourself from the confines of a pie plate is so liberating. Somehow, no matter how a galette slumps, breaks, or browns, it's always beautiful. Glory lies in irregularity. Unlike a deep fruit pie, which tends to harbor too much liquid, galettes always leak a little bit. Rest easy. That's a good thing! It seems to me that exactly the right amount of liquid creeps out so that what's left inside is a nicely thickened fruit filling with sweet, concentrated flavor, and a crisp bottom crust. The secret is to remove it from the parchment paper while it's still warm and the leaked juices haven't solidified. A bonus is that galettes cool much faster than pies. You are closer to dessert bliss than you think.

Prepare the pastry: Whisk together the flour, granulated sugar, and salt in a large bowl. Cut in the butter with a pastry blender or 2 knives until the mixture resembles even, coarse sand without big pieces. You can use your fingers to rub the butter into the flour to get a more even distribution, but be sure to chill the mixture for a few minutes before proceeding if the butter has gotten warm. Add the ice water to the mixture and stir with a fork until a shaggy dough forms. Add 1 or 2 more tablespoons of water if you need to, but stop before the dough gets too wet. It should just hold together when squeezed. (Feel free to do this in a food processor if you have one. Just use a light hand to process the butter and water in. It can be easy to overwork the dough in the processor.)

Using your hands, gather the dough into a rough ball in the bowl. Put a piece of plastic wrap on the countertop and place the dough on it. Wrap the dough and flatten it into a small rectangle. Refrigerate until cold, about 2 hours or up to 2 days. Alternatively, freeze the dough, well wrapped, for up to 1 month.

Prepare the jam: In a small saucepan, combine the cherries and granulated sugar and cook over medium heat, crushing the fruit with a potato masher, until the fruit is soft and some of the liquid has evaporated, about 10 minutes. Remove a few tablespoons of the cherry juice and mix it with the cornstarch to make a slurry. Add the slurry to the pot and continue to cook, stirring, until the jam is thick, about 2 minutes. Remove from the heat and let cool completely.

(continued on next page)

PASTRY:

1¼ cups all-purpose flour, plus more for dusting

2 tablespoons granulated sugar

¾ teaspoon kosher salt

10 tablespoons/1¼ sticks cold unsalted butter, cut into pieces

¼ cup ice water, plus more if needed

SOUR CHERRY JAM:

12 ounces sour cherries, pitted (2 cups)

¼ cup granulated sugar

1 teaspoon cornstarch

FILLING:

1 pound nectarines, pitted and cut into ¼- to ½-inch wedges (about 3 cups)

¼ cup granulated sugar

1 tablespoon freshly squeezed lemon juice

1 tablespoon cornstarch

TO FINISH:

1 large egg, lightly beaten

Sanding sugar for sprinkling (optional)

When ready to assemble the galette, preheat the oven to 400°F.

Prepare the filling: Toss the nectarines wedges with the granulated sugar, lemon juice, and cornstarch. On a lightly floured piece of parchment paper, roll the dough into a 12 x 9-inch rectangle. Spread the jam in an even layer on the dough, leaving a 1½-inch border bare on all sides. Shingle the nectarines over the jam in 3 rows. Fold the 4 edges of the pastry up and over the fruit and press it gently.

Using the parchment paper, carefully transfer the galette to a rimmed baking sheet. Brush the edges with the beaten egg and sprinkle with sanding sugar (if using). Bake until the filling is bubbling and the crust is deep golden brown, about 45 minutes. Transfer the baking sheet to a wire rack and let the galette cool at room temperature for 15 minutes, then carefully use a long offset spatula to loosen the bottom of the crust from the parchment paper and slide it onto the rack or serving plate. Serve warm or room temperature.

Raspberry Crostata with Hazelnut Graham Crust

SERVES 8

My new supermarket featured a glossy portrait of Biggie Smalls in a gilded frame, but little in the way of fresh fruit. Those early days in New York City required some improvising. Just weeks earlier, my friend Juliet and I had graduated from college in Ohio. Now our apartment was full of mice, leaks, and mysterious odors. Chicken bones, licked clean, littered our stoop every morning. Sticking to my baking routine was the only way I knew to make it a home.

Every week, I froze a disk of homemade pie dough. On Saturday mornings, I visited our run-down Met supermarket and picked through the mealy apples and moldy berries to find the fruit for a simple crostata. Something always worked out. Mo' pie, no problems.

Prepare the crust: Whisk together the all-purpose flour, graham flour, hazelnut meal, granulated sugar, and salt in a large bowl. Cut the butter in with a pastry blender or 2 knives until the mixture resembles even, coarse sand with a few tiny pebbles. You can use your fingers to rub the butter into the flour to get a more even distribution, but be sure to chill the mixture for a few minutes before proceeding if the butter has gotten warm. Add the ice water to the mixture and stir with a fork until a shaggy dough forms. Add 1 or 2 more tablespoons of water if you need to, but stop before the dough gets too wet. It should just hold together when squeezed. (You could also make this dough in a food processor.)

Using your hands, gather the dough into a rough ball in the bowl. Put a piece of plastic wrap on the countertop and place the dough on it. Wrap the dough and flatten it into a 6-inch disk. Refrigerate until cold, about 2 hours or up to 2 days. Alternatively, freeze the dough, well wrapped, for up to 1 month.

When ready to prepare the crostata, preheat the oven to 375°F.

Prepare the filling: In a large bowl, gently toss together the raspberries, granulated sugar, lemon zest, cornstarch, and salt.

On a lightly floured, large piece of parchment paper, using a lightly floured rolling pin, roll out the dough to a 12-inch circle. Set the parchment and the dough onto a rimmed baking sheet. If the dough has gotten soft at this point, pop it in the freezer for a few minutes until it becomes firm enough to work with but not frozen. Mound the filling in the center of the dough, leaving a 3- to 4-inch border bare on all sides. Fold the edges of the pastry up and around the filling, moving any runny filling back to the center,

(continued on next page)

CRUST:

½ cup all-purpose flour, plus more for dusting

½ cup graham or whole wheat flour

⅓ cup hazelnut meal

2 tablespoons granulated sugar

½ teaspoon kosher salt

10 tablespoons/1¼ sticks cold unsalted butter, cut into small pieces

3 tablespoons ice water, plus more if needed

FILLING:

1 pound fresh raspberries (about 3 cups)

⅓ cup granulated sugar

½ teaspoon finely grated lemon zest

1 tablespoon cornstarch

Pinch of kosher salt

TO FINISH:

1 large egg, beaten

Sanding sugar for sprinkling

2 tablespoons cold unsalted butter, cut into small pieces

and pleating the dough as needed to seal. Put the crostata on the sheet in the freezer and freeze for 10 minutes.

Brush the top of the pastry and the edges with the beaten egg. Sprinkle with sanding sugar. Top the filling with the butter. Bake until the crust is golden brown and the raspberry filling is bubbling, 45 to 55 minutes. (Crostatas tend to spring a few leaks, so don't worry if that happens.) Transfer the baking sheet to a wire rack to cool slightly before serving the crostata with a big scoop of vanilla ice cream.

Whole-Grain Chocolate Chip Cookies

MAKES ABOUT 3 DOZEN COOKIES

My new apartment has a wine fridge in the kitchen. Most people would assume that a single mom would praise the heavens for a wine fridge. Not this one. Liquid courage is not my thing. It took exactly one experience of caring for an infant while nursing a hangover to recognize that I would rather eat my kombucha mother slathered with mayonnaise than drink too much ever again. So, I've discovered a better use for my wine fridge. The little pull-out shelves are the perfect size for different kinds of flour, nuts, seeds, and coconut. Eggs and butter fit in there, too. It isn't as cold as the main fridge, so they are ready for baking even faster.

When it comes down to it, a warm, soft-centered chocolate chip cookie with crunchy, caramelized edges and pools of deep, dark chocolate is just as intoxicating and comforting as anything else. Chocolate disks, if you can find them, make much better chocolate chip cookies than do chips. They're wide and flat and create lovely chocolate strata within the cookies.

I like to freeze portioned scoops of this dough and have it in the freezer at all times. A warm cookie should always be close at hand.

In a medium bowl, whisk together the whole wheat and spelt flours, baking soda, salt, and baking powder. In a large bowl, with an electric mixer on medium speed, beat the butter, granulated sugar, and brown sugar together until fluffy, about 2 minutes. Add the eggs, 1 at a time, and then add the vanilla. Reduce the mixer speed to low, add the flour mixture and the chocolate disks, and mix just until combined. Cover the dough with plastic wrap and refrigerate for at least 1 hour or up to 3 days.

Preheat the oven to 350°F. Line 2 rimmed baking sheets with parchment paper.

Scoop the dough into balls that are 3 tablespoons (1½ ounces) each and roll into neat circles, spacing them 3 inches apart on the prepared baking sheets. Bake the cookies, 1 sheet at a time, until they are golden brown and the tops are set with a hint of wetness underneath, 14 to 16 minutes. Transfer the baking sheet to a wire rack to cool for a few minutes, then transfer the individual cookies to the rack to cool completely. Repeat with the remaining dough.

Store the cookies in an airtight container at room temperature for 2 days and in the freezer for up to a month.

2 cups whole wheat flour

1½ cups spelt flour

1¼ teaspoons baking soda

1¼ teaspoons kosher salt

1 teaspoon baking powder

1 cup/2 sticks unsalted butter, at room temperature

1¼ cups granulated sugar

1 cup packed dark brown sugar

2 large eggs, at room temperature

1 tablespoon pure vanilla extract

12 ounces bittersweet chocolate disks or chips (about 2½ cups)

Sweet Potato Cinnamon Buns
with Browned Butter Cream Cheese Glaze

MAKES 10 BUNS

My son loves my sweet potato soup. I feel as if I just won ten James Beard Awards from this tiny critic who would always rather be eating yogurt. He looked at the spoon tentatively before the first bite. I could practically see the thought bubble pop up beside his head. "This is *orange*?! No thank you, Mama." I persisted and he opened his mouth. He slurped, nodded, and opened his mouth right back up again. We did it again. And again. I couldn't help but kiss his round cheeks in between each bite. He was eating my food. He liked it. And it was good for him.

In my acceptance speeches, I will have to thank these sweet potato cinnamon buns. While working on the recipe, I had roasted so many extra potatoes that I had to find another use for them. Like my baby, I love sweet potatoes in all forms, but I'm especially fond of adding them to sweet breads. They add flavor and give them a pillow-soft texture. Swirled with cinnamon and topped with luscious cream cheese glaze, these guys made for a lovely indulgence after such a nutritious lunch.

DOUGH:

½ cup whole milk

6 tablespoons/¾ stick unsalted butter, cut into small pieces, plus more for bowl and skillet

1 large egg, at room temperature

½ cup roasted and puréed sweet potato flesh (from 1 potato)

3 cups all-purpose flour, plus more for dusting, if necessary

⅓ cup packed dark brown sugar

2¼ teaspoons active dry yeast

½ teaspoon kosher salt

CINNAMON FILLING:

¼ cup packed dark brown sugar

2 tablespoons ground cinnamon

Prepare the dough: In a small pot, bring the milk just to a boil over medium heat. Watch closely to ensure that the milk doesn't boil over. Remove from the heat and add the butter to the pot to melt. Transfer the mixture to a small bowl and let it cool to 110° to 115°F. (It should be warm to the touch, but not too hot.) Add the egg and sweet potato purée and stir to combine.

In the bowl of a stand mixer fitted with the paddle attachment, or in a large bowl and using a wooden spoon, combine the flour, brown sugar, yeast, and salt. Add the warm milk mixture and mix just until incorporated.

Switch to the dough hook and knead the dough on low speed (or knead with your hands) until smooth and elastic, about 8 minutes. Form the dough into a ball and transfer it to a buttered bowl, cover it, and leave it in a warm, draft-free spot until it has doubled in size, 1 to 2 hours.

Prepare the cinnamon filling: Mix together the brown sugar, cinnamon, and salt in a small bowl. Add the butter and mash to combine. Cover with plastic wrap and set aside.

Prepare the pepita filling: Melt the butter in a 12-inch cast-iron skillet over medium-low heat. Add the pepitas and salt and cook until lightly browned and popping, 2 to 3 minutes. Sprinkle with the brown sugar and cook, stirring, until the sugar has melted and coated the pepitas, 1 to 2 minutes. Transfer to a plate to cool. Wipe the skillet out with a paper towel and let cool. (continued on page 44)

½ teaspoon kosher salt

3 tablespoons unsalted butter, at room temperature

PEPITA FILLING:

1 tablespoon unsalted butter

3½ ounces pepitas (⅔ cup)

¼ teaspoon kosher salt

¼ cup packed dark brown sugar

GLAZE:

4 tablespoons/½ stick unsalted butter

2 ounces cream cheese, at room temperature

¼ cup packed dark brown sugar

½ teaspoon pure vanilla extract

Pinch of kosher salt

2 to 4 tablespoons whole milk, at room temperature

Butter the cast-iron pan. Tip out the dough onto a very lightly floured work surface. Roll it into a 12 x 11-inch rectangle. Spread the cinnamon filling evenly over the surface. Break up the sugared pepitas into smaller pieces and sprinkle over the cinnamon filling. Tightly roll up the dough and pinch the top seam closed. With a serrated knife, cut the roll crosswise into 10 equal pieces. Set them in the pan, spirals facing upward. Cover loosely with plastic wrap and let them rest until the dough has almost doubled again, 1 to 1½ hours.

Preheat the oven to 350°F. Uncover the rolls and bake until golden brown and puffed and an instant-read thermometer inserted into the center reads 185° to 190°F, about 20 to 25 minutes.

Meanwhile, prepare the glaze: Cook the butter in a small skillet over medium heat until the milk solids have turned golden brown and the butter smells nutty, about 6 minutes. Transfer to a medium bowl and chill in the freezer until cool and just beginning to solidify.

Beat the chilled butter, cream cheese, brown sugar, vanilla, and salt until smooth. Add the milk, 1 tablespoon at a time, until it is exactly as thick as you like it.

Transfer the buns to a wire rack to cool for 5 minutes, then top with glaze. Let cool slightly before serving.

Strawberry Rhubarb Cake with Bay and Orange

SERVES 8

Instagram would have you believe that rhubarb practically arranges itself into flaming pink chevron patterns on top of cakes that stay gorgeous even after baking and slicing. I have never found that to be true. The reality of baking with rhubarb is that it most often loses its gorgeous color and turns greenish brown with hints of mauve. Or the cake beneath it rises up and envelops the fruit. It's not exactly ugly, but unless excessive care is taken, it's not exceptionally gorgeous. And really, who has time for excessive care just for the sake of looks?

But isn't that just Instagram in a nutshell? How many times have I seen happy, fat babies dressed in stain-free, hand wash–only onesies, snuggled by parents who are not only lovers but best friends, seated in gorgeous tiled kitchens, nary a dirty dish in sight, eating spinach.

My rhubarb cake is like my life. It's not picture perfect. It's messy and a bit haphazard, but it's really, really good. The strawberries and rhubarb melt together into a caramel-scented jammy sludge. The butter cake underneath sops up all of those flavorful juices. The spelt flour adds a whole-meal nuttiness and the bay leaves a slightly unexpected, savory edge.

Preheat the oven to 350°F. Butter a 9-inch-diameter, 2-inch-high round baking pan and line it with parchment. Butter the parchment.

Infuse the butter: Melt the butter and the bay leaves in a small saucepan over medium heat. Let the mixture simmer together for about 1 minute. Transfer the butter mixture to a large bowl and let it stand until cool and semisolid, at least 1 hour. (Pop the bowl into the fridge to speed things along, but don't let it get it so cold that you won't be able to cream it easily with the sugar.)

Meanwhile, prepare the topping: Toss the rhubarb and strawberries with the cornstarch. Spread the fruit mixture evenly over the bottom of the prepared pan. Place 1 tablespoon of water in a small saucepan. Sprinkle the sugar over the water so that it is evenly moistened. Bring the mixture to a simmer over medium heat and cook, swirling the pan occasionally, until the mixture is amber colored, about 3 minutes. Don't let the caramel become too dark now as it will continue to darken in the oven, but don't remove it from the heat until it has some nice color. The amber color indicates good caramel flavor. Remove the pot from the heat and swirl in the butter and salt. Drizzle the caramel evenly over the fruit in the pan.

(continued on next page)

CAKE:

¾ cup/1½ sticks unsalted butter, plus more for pan

6 fresh bay leaves, crushed

2 cups spelt flour

1½ teaspoons baking powder

¾ teaspoon kosher salt

¼ teaspoon baking soda

¾ cup granulated sugar

1½ teaspoons finely grated orange zest

3 large eggs, at room temperature

½ cup whole-milk plain yogurt, at room temperature

TOPPING:

10 ounces rhubarb, cut into 1-inch pieces (about 2 cups)

8 ounces hulled and halved strawberries (quartered if large) (about 1½ cups)

2 teaspoons cornstarch

½ cup granulated sugar

4 tablespoons/ ½ stick unsalted butter, cut into pieces, at room temperature

Pinch of kosher salt

Ice cream or whipped cream for serving

Finish preparing the cake: In a medium bowl, whisk together the flour, baking powder, salt, and baking soda.

Remove the bay leaves from the butter, making sure to scrape all the butter back into the bowl, and discard them. With an electric mixer on medium speed, beat the butter, sugar, and orange zest until pale and fluffy, about 3 minutes. Add the eggs, 1 at a time, beating after each addition until fully combined. Add half of the flour mixture and beat to combine. Then, add the yogurt and beat to combine. Beat in the remaining flour mixture. Top the prepared fruit with the batter and smooth the top.

Bake until a toothpick inserted into the center of the cake comes out with moist crumbs attached, 50 to 60 minutes. Tent the top of the cake with foil if it is browning too quickly. Transfer in the pan to a wire rack to cool for 10 minutes, then carefully flip the cake onto a serving plate. (Don't forget to scrape out the juices.) Serve at room temperature with ice cream or a dollop of whipped cream.

CHAPTER TWO

GRACE

Paper Birds

In 2001, my dressiest pants were a pair of gold velour bell-bottoms. Utterly misguided fancy pants. I wore them on two special occasions. The first time was the *Rent* audition I stumbled through that still sends goosebumps of embarrassment up and down my arms. I went with an Erykah Badu song. And I did not get a callback, believe it or not. The second time was my first postcollege job interview for a grown-up position with benefits. Somehow the pants didn't immediately disqualify me, and I got the job.

I became a program coordinator for a website called Idealist. Our offices were on the sixty-sixth floor of the Empire State Building. Walking into the iconic building every morning, edging my way through a sea of suits and skirts, catching glimpses of my reflection on the mirrored walls—it all made me feel as if I were playing the lead in the movie of my life. Proud. Thrilled. Hopeful beyond measure and sense.

I shared a little office with my boss, Lorene. She was by the window, and I was wedged into the opposite corner, facing a beige wall. I didn't mind. If I looked over her shoulder, I had that view of New York City. That view. On my very first week, when the work had yet to accumulate, I spent more time staring out the window than doing anything else.

One afternoon, Lorene stepped out for lunch. I took the opportunity to sneak over to her side of the office and gaze out the window. The city looked tiny. Neat rows of gray blocks with ants and toy cars weaving up and down the dark pathways. Through the rose-colored haze of newfound employment, New York looked conquerable.

And then it occurred to me that the windows of the sixty-sixth floor of the Empire State Building were made to open. There was no lock, no screen, no word of warning. *How about a little fresh air?* I thought.

I should have known. But I didn't know. The window slid right up, without any extra effort that might have alerted me to a possible problem. The instant I lifted the glass, I felt a terrifying pull, and watched, eyes as wide as golf balls, as every loose piece of paper on Lorene's desk was instantaneously sucked out into the sky. Flying papers actually smacked me in the face on their way out. I struggled to close the window and watched through the glass as my boss's work floated out across New York City, fluttering in the wind like a slow-moving flock of birds. I sat back down at my desk and waited for Lorene to return from lunch.

As it happens, Lorene is a saint. When she came back, I told her what I had done. She smiled and shrugged, "If it was anything important, I'm sure I have a copy." The insanity of that response still befuddles me. I guess she didn't want to break my spirit on my first week as a working woman. I am still so grateful to her.

Lorene, if you're reading this, I want to take this opportunity to apologize. Again and again. Thank you for your patience. My self-assigned penance is to cut sixty perfect squares of parchment paper, tiny versions of those papers I lost eighteen years ago. Within each of those paper propitiations, I will wrap a dark chocolate caramel. A sweet gift with just an edge of bitter that requires some thoughtful chewing, as I imagine the job of being my boss did way back then.

Salted Chocolate-Covered Chocolate Caramels

MAKES ABOUT 60 CARAMELS

These make a perfect apology. They wrap up pretty and neat. And they take a while to chew, which keeps the wronged party busy while you make your escape.

Neutral oil, such as safflower, for pan and knife

1 cup heavy cream

4 tablespoons/ ½ stick unsalted butter, cut into pieces

6 ounces bittersweet chocolate (not chips), chopped (about 1½ cups)

1 cup granulated sugar

½ cup light corn syrup

½ teaspoon kosher salt

CHOCOLATE COATING:

8 ounces bittersweet chocolate (not chips), chopped (about 2 cups)

TO FINISH:

Flaky sea salt for sprinkling (optional)

Prepare the caramels: Lightly oil an 8-inch square baking pan. Line the pan with parchment paper, leaving a 2-inch overhang on 2 opposite sides. Lightly oil the parchment.

In a small pot, heat the cream and butter over medium heat until the butter is melted. Add the chocolate and let stand for 2 minutes. Alternatively, melt in the microwave in a microwave-safe bowl. Whisk until smooth and set aside.

In a medium saucepan over medium-high heat, combine the sugar, corn syrup, salt, and ¼ cup of water and heat until the sugar turns deep amber, swirling the pan to caramelize the sugar evenly, 10 to 12 minutes. Do not stir the mixture. Remove from the heat and add the chocolate mixture. Be careful: this will bubble up and sputter. Stir until smooth. Add the salt.

Attach a candy thermometer to the side of the pot and return the pan to the heat. Cook the mixture over medium heat until the candy thermometer reads between 248° and 250°F, 8 to 12 minutes, stirring constantly. Pour into the prepared pan but do not scrape out anything that clings to the pan. Let cool at room temperature until firm, at least 2 hours.

Cut around the parchment-free edges to release the caramel from the pan. Using the parchment overhang on either side, lift the block of caramel out of the baking pan and set on a cutting board. Cut into 1-inch squares with a long, sharp knife. Oil the knife as necessary.

Prepare the chocolate coating: Line a baking sheet with parchment paper. In a medium heatproof bowl, melt the 8 ounces of chocolate in short bursts in the microwave or over a double boiler. (See page 7 for directions on tempering chocolate if you'd like to go the extra step.) Using 2 forks, dip each caramel in the melted chocolate and swirl it around to coat. Tap each candy against the edge of the bowl a few times to release any excess chocolate. Transfer the chocolate-covered caramels to the prepared pan. Sprinkle with the flaky sea salt (if using). Chill for about 30 minutes to set the chocolate.

As the caramels chill, cut sixty 4-inch squares of parchment paper. Wrap each of the caramels in a square of paper. Store the caramels in an airtight container in the fridge for up to 2 weeks.

SLEEP, SAMMY. SLEEP.

After we had all stuffed ourselves with bagels and clementines, we lolled around Juliet's living room, chatting and hanging out the way friends who have known each other for twenty years can. No much talking but a lot of laughing.

Juliet's son Asa climbed into my lap for about three delicious seconds. At two years old, he had juicy cheeks, tousled sandy blond hair, and adorable Tic Tac–size teeth that flashed when he grinned. For those few moments, I let down my guard. I let his sweet scent get to me. I put my arms around his tiny body and hugged for as long as he would let me. I was delirious with pleasure. He wriggled out as fast as he'd wriggled in.

The adults were talking mortgage rates and mold inspections, and Asa found a friend in me. He said, in his lispy, raspy peanut voice, "Sleep, Sammy. Sleep." I closed my eyes dutifully, lay my head down, and pretended to sleep. He wobbled out of the room, then ran back in, and smooshed his fat little face as hard as he could against mine. "Wake up!" he giggled. Then again. "Sleep, Sammy. Sleep." We played the game over and over again.

In the past, I wouldn't have played this game. *Maybe Sam wants to read you a story* was a sentence that filled my heart with the darkest dread. I never wanted to read to someone else's child. Ever. My friends' sweet cherubs would waddle over to me for a hug, face smeared with traces of hummus and avocado, and I would turn away. I made a point of visiting my girl-friends after their babies had already gone to sleep. Just missed him, huh? Too bad.

I'm ashamed to admit to the cold face I put on for years. The manufactured lack of interest and diligent avoidance. My favorite people were taking on one of life's biggest challenges and I pretended not to care. It hurt too much to care.

I've never had a moment of ambiguity about becoming a mother. So, when my husband admitted that he didn't want to be a father, I was crushed. In those same years, my closest friends were becoming mothers. I seethed with plain old, ugly jealousy. The embarrassment and shame of feeling envious of people that I loved added to the pain of wanting everything they had.

Then, my husband and I split. The issues couldn't be resolved. I found myself desperately sad. It's one thing to lose a partner. But with that partner I also lost the immediate opportunity to have a child. At thirty-five years old, I knew that I wasn't too old to make a new life, but the steps I had to take to do it seemed impossibly huge. All the while, it seemed that my friends were living their best lives. New babies. Happy marriages. Homes full of love.

In an effort to protect myself from their bliss, I turned away from them. I avoided a baby shower getaway weekend with my most dear girlfriends because I couldn't face their joy. I visited new babies sparingly. I couldn't even muster the strength to ask my friends how they were coping with their new roles.

And somehow they all loved me still.

My husband and I got back together. We decided to have a baby. And then he left again. But my friends were always there. They offered to throw me a baby shower. And they told me exactly which baby shampoo to add to my baby registry. And they held my hand during sonograms and laughed with me when the technician pointed out that the baby was snuggling my placenta like a pillow. They scanned apartment listings to help me find one for me and the baby that would be cozy, affordable, and have fewer than six flights of stairs. They came over in 95-degree heat to help me assemble a particularly unruly travel crib. They climbed the ladder when I was too big and hung the tiny felt mobile over the changing table. They found the perfect used bookshelf for the nursery and helped me bribe the store clerk to bring it to my house. And I have let down my wall.

I was a terrible friend. I was a conditional friend. And in response, my people gave all their love to me and my baby. Unconditional friendship. I could drown in the pleasure of their families and their love.

So, now I turn to the kitchen and consider a baking project to convey something that I couldn't over those years. My apologies aren't quite enough. I need a treat that's tender and delicious. Comforting and just sweet enough. Scones. Even their preparation encourages friendship. Some baked goods take patience and concentration. Not scones. Dump the dry ingredients in a bowl. Crush in the cold butter with your fingers. Stir in the liquid with a fork. Pat-pat, shape, cut, and you're done. I can do that work with my hands, while my mind and heart are truly focused on the friend I've invited over to talk. Step one: ask her how she's doing and really listen to the answer.

Warm from the oven, the crunchy exteriors and downy centers should be enjoyed casually. No pretense. No forks. We break off pieces while we stand around the warm oven, sipping tea, talking it all out. And when she has to leave too soon, I wrap the leftovers in a foil packet and tuck them into my beloved friend's purse. It's a hidden treasure for the gal whose eyes are tired from too little sleep but whose heart did not hesitate to offer kindness upon kindness when I needed it the most.

Banana Bread Scones

MAKES 8 SCONES

These scones are the perfect breakfast when you're rich in overripe bananas but don't have the time or patience for banana bread. They bake up fast and don't need to cool before being eaten. Some of the butter might ooze out a little while they bake, but don't worry. That just helps get the bottom extra crunchy.

Preheat the oven to 425°F.

In a small bowl, whisk together the banana, cream, egg, and vanilla. In a large bowl, whisk together the flour, brown sugar, baking powder, and salt.

Cut in the butter with a pastry blender, or 2 knives used like scissors, until the mixture resembles coarse meal with some larger pieces. (You can use your fingers if you work fast enough that the butter stays cold.) Toss in the chopped chocolate and hazelnuts.

Drizzle in the banana mixture and stir with a fork until the mixture is crumbly and moistened, but stop before you've mixed it into a uniform batter. Tip out the mixture onto a parchment-lined baking sheet and pat it into a 6-inch circle. Using a sharp knife or a bench scraper, cut the circle into 8 equal triangles. (At this point, you could freeze the triangles well-wrapped on their sheet for another day. Bake them from frozen.) Spread the triangles apart and brush the tops with the cream. Sprinkle with sanding sugar.

Bake until the scones are golden brown and set, about 22 minutes. A toothpick inserted into the center of a scone should come out clean. Transfer the baking sheet to a wire rack to cool slightly. Serve warm or room temperature. Scones are best the day they're made.

1 extra-large, extra-ripe banana, mashed (½ cup)

⅓ cup heavy cream, plus more for brushing

1 large egg, lightly beaten

1 teaspoon pure vanilla extract

2 cups all-purpose flour

⅓ cup packed dark brown sugar

2½ teaspoons baking powder

½ teaspoon kosher salt

½ cup/1 stick cold unsalted butter, cut into pieces

2¼ ounces semisweet chocolate, chopped (½ cup)

1¼ ounces hazelnuts, toasted, skinned, and finely chopped (about ¼ cup)

Sanding sugar for sprinkling

Cherry Ricotta Turnovers

MAKES 8 TURNOVERS

Working with phyllo dough is the perfect occasion for letting go of any judgment about yourself and your skills. First, it must be said that buying frozen phyllo, instead of making it from scratch, is perfectly acceptable. You'll never catch any shade from me. Second, it is exceptionally forgiving. Yes, it rips. It folds over onto itself. It looks messy. But if you just slather each layer with butter, the whole thing will come together like a dream. And the ragged bits only add to the beauty of the final product. Just let the praise roll in. You deserve it.

These pies work best if the ricotta is dry. If your ricotta is wet, drain it in some cheesecloth set over a bowl in the fridge for an hour or two before assembling the filling.

½ cup well-drained ricotta cheese

¼ cup confectioners' sugar

1 large egg yolk

½ teaspoon pure vanilla extract

¼ teaspoon ground cinnamon

Pinch of ground cloves

16 sheets phyllo, thawed (from a 1-pound box)

½ cup/1 stick unsalted butter, melted

Granulated sugar for sprinkling

4½ ounces sweet cherries, pitted and chopped (about ½ cup)

Honey for drizzling (optional)

Preheat the oven to 375°F. Line 2 rimmed baking sheets with parchment paper.

In a small bowl, fold together the ricotta, confectioners' sugar, egg yolk, vanilla, cinnamon, and cloves.

Cut the 16 phyllo sheets lengthwise into 4½-inch-wide strips. Cover with a barely damp towel while you work.

Set a strip on a work surface, with the long side facing you, and brush the entire strip with melted butter. Sprinkle evenly with granulated sugar, then top with another strip. Brush the top with butter. Top with 1 tablespoon of the ricotta filling and 1 tablespoon of the cherries in the center about 1 inch from the left-side end. Gently pull the top left corner down, over the filling, to meet the bottom edge and form a triangle. Butter the top of the triangle.

Now, gently grab the bottom left corner and lift it up to meet the top edge and wrap the triangle one more time. Brush the top with butter. Continue to fold the corners, as you would fold a flag, buttering every dry surface, until the sheet is completely folded into a large triangle. Transfer to 1 of the prepared baking sheets. Repeat with the remaining phyllo, butter, sugar, and filling.

Sprinkle the turnovers with granulated sugar. With a sharp paring knife, cut a small slit in the top of each turnover, taking care not to pierce through to the other side. Bake until puffed and deep golden brown, about 25 minutes. Let cool for a few minutes before serving. Drizzle with honey to serve, if you like.

Coffee Crème Bundt Cake

SERVES 10 TO 12

My dad drinks instant coffee that he first "brews" in the microwave and then dilutes with overflowing spoonfuls of condensed milk. As a youthful coffee snob, I turned up my nose and insisted that what he drank wasn't *real* coffee. But as I've gotten older and become less of a jerk, I've realized that what's cool doesn't matter when it's delicious. My dad's morning cup, supersweet and creamy with just a hint of coffee, is damn good. And now, I always ask him to make me one, too.

This glorious coffee-flavored Bundt is more sweet than coffee and has a gooey, condensed milk glaze that you may have to resist eating with a spoon.

Preheat the oven to 350°F. Butter and flour a 12-cup Bundt cake pan.

In a medium bowl, whisk together the flour, cardamom, baking powder, salt, and baking soda. In a large bowl, combine the vanilla and espresso powder. Add the dark brown sugar, granulated sugar, and butter and beat with an electric mixer on medium speed until fluffy, about 4 minutes. Beat in the eggs, 1 at a time, scraping down the sides of the bowl as necessary, until well combined.

Reduce the speed to low and alternate adding the flour mixture and the sour cream, starting and ending with the flour mixture, and mix until just combined. Transfer the batter to the prepared pan and smooth the top. Bake until puffed and set and a skewer inserted into the center comes out with moist crumbs attached, 50 to 55 minutes. Transfer the cake to a wire rack to cool for about 15 minutes, then flip out the cake onto the rack to cool completely.

Prepare the glaze: In a small saucepan, heat the condensed milk, butter, egg yolk, salt, and espresso powder over medium-low heat, stirring constantly, until thickened, about 4 minutes. Drizzle the warm glaze over the cooled cake. Top with the walnuts. Serve warm or at room temperature.

CAKE:

1¼ cups/2½ sticks unsalted butter, at room temperature, plus more for pan

2½ cups all-purpose flour, plus more for pan

2 teaspoons freshly ground cardamom

1½ teaspoons baking powder

¾ teaspoon kosher salt

¼ teaspoon baking soda

1 tablespoon pure vanilla extract

3 tablespoons instant espresso powder

¾ cup packed dark brown sugar

¾ cup granulated sugar

3 large eggs, at room temperature

¾ cup sour cream

GLAZE:

¾ cup sweetened condensed milk

2 tablespoons unsalted butter

1 large egg yolk

½ teaspoon kosher salt

¼ teaspoon instant espresso powder

2¼ ounces walnuts, chopped (½ cup)

Crème Brûlée Tart with Pears and Chocolate

SERVES 8 TO 10

A friend once told me that I was endlessly surprising. I think it's one of the most satisfying compliments anyone has ever paid me. I hope he meant it. It's taken me half a lifetime to cut myself a little slack, but it turns out that the things that make me surprising make me special, flaws included. (Duh, right?) I'd take surprising over perfect any day. And I want my life to be the same.

I created this tart with his words in mind. Upon first glance, you see sparkling caramelized sugar, rendered smooth with a kitchen torch. But under that crisp layer are many more: a vanilla-flecked custard and a silky chocolate cream, and fresh pears set in a browned crust. Gorgeous to look at and an unexpected journey for the taste buds.

You want pears that are ripe but not on the verge of collapse. I like baking with Comice pears because of their creamy flesh and excellent flavor, but you could use medium-ripe Bartletts as well.

CRUST:
1¼ cups all-purpose flour, plus more for dusting cup

½ cup confectioners' sugar

½ teaspoon kosher salt

½ cup/1 stick cold unsalted butter, cut into pieces

1 large egg yolk

2 to 4 teaspoons cold water

CHOCOLATE AND PEAR LAYER:
2¼ ounces bittersweet chocolate, chopped (½ cup)

¼ cup heavy cream

1 large egg yolk

¼ teaspoon kosher salt

2 medium-ripe Comice pears (9 to 10 ounces each), peeled, cored, and sliced ⅛ inch thick

Prepare the crust: In a food processor, combine the flour, confectioners' sugar, and salt. Add the butter and pulse until the mixture is the texture of coarse meal with some larger, pea-size pieces. Add the egg yolk and 2 teaspoons of the cold water and pulse until the mixture is evenly moistened and holds together when you squeeze a bit in your hands. Add up to 2 teaspoons more water but take care not to make the dough too wet. It should still look sandy, not clumpy.

Tip out the dough into a 9-inch fluted tart pan with a removable bottom and spread it out evenly. Using the bottom of a small measuring cup dipped in flour, if necessary, press the dough into the bottom and sides of the pan to make an even crust. Wrap with plastic wrap and freeze for at least 20 minutes. Preheat the oven to 375°F.

Set the frozen crust on a rimmed baking sheet, line it with parchment, and fill it with pie weights or dried beans. Bake until the crust is set and dry, under the parchment, about 25 minutes. Remove the parchment and beans and bake until the crust is golden brown, another 15 to 20 minutes, tenting the edges with foil if they begin to get too dark.

Meanwhile, prepare the chocolate and pear layer: Place the chocolate in a heatproof bowl. Heat the cream in a small saucepan over medium heat until it just starts to bubble around the edges, pour it over the chocolate, and let it stand for 1 minute. Whisk until smooth, then whisk in the egg yolk

VANILLA LAYER:

½ cup heavy cream

2 tablespoons whole milk

3 large egg yolks

Seeds scraped from ½ vanilla bean, or ¾ teaspoon pure vanilla extract

2 tablespoons granulated sugar

Pinch of kosher salt

TO FINISH:

2 to 3 tablespoons granulated sugar

and the salt. Transfer the chocolate mixture to the warm crust and smooth it out into an even layer. Top with the pears in an overlapping, decorative spiral.

Prepare the custard layer: In a small bowl, whisk together the cream, milk, egg yolks, vanilla bean seeds, granulated sugar, and salt. Pour over the pears. Lower the oven temperature to 325°F and bake the tart until the custard is just set, 35 to 40 minutes. Transfer to a wire rack to cool slightly, then transfer to the fridge to cool for at least 2 hours. (If you're holding the tart longer at this stage, cover it with plastic wrap after 2 hours.)

To serve, sprinkle the granulated sugar evenly over the top of the tart. Using a mini blowtorch held about 2 inches from the top of the tart, evenly melt the sugar until deep golden brown and bubbling. Let stand for 5 minutes, then serve immediately.

Danish Sugar Cookies with Currants and Lemon

MAKES ABOUT 3 DOZEN COOKIES

Our house was always stocked with a blue tin of Danish butter cookies. Frilly they were not, unless you count the white paper cups they came in. The whole family loved them, my brother most of all. He saw value no one else did, appeal that went beyond the sandy, slightly salty sweets. He used to keep his money in the old blue cookie tin. It may have been thrifty, but all I could focus on was the embarrassing rattle that accompanied our walks around the mall. Back then, I thought he was nuts. Now I see that was a part of a wonderful weirdness, and a comfort with himself, that I want to hold on to forever. These little sweeties are for him.

In a large bowl, with an electric mixer on medium speed, beat the butter and granulated sugar until combined and creamy, about 3 minutes. Add the egg, lemon zest, and vanilla and beat until combined. Beat in the flour, currants, baking soda, and salt until just combined.

Preheat the oven to 350°F.

Line a rimmed baking sheet with parchment paper. Transfer about one quarter of the dough to a piping bag fitted with a ½-inch star tip. Pipe small rings, about 1¾ inches in diameter, onto the prepared baking sheet. Repeat with the remaining dough. Freeze until firm, about 20 minutes.

Line 2 rimmed baking sheets with parchment paper. Tip a little bit of sanding sugar into a small bowl. Quickly dip the cookies into the sugar to coat, then transfer them, about 1 inch apart, to the prepared baking sheets. Return the remaining cookies to the freezer.

Bake the cookies until golden around the edges, 13 to 18 minutes, rotating the sheets halfway through baking. Transfer the baking sheet to a wire rack to cool. Repeat with the remaining cookies.

Keep the cookies in an airtight container at room temperature for 3 days or in the freezer for up to 2 months.

1 cup/2 sticks unsalted butter, at room temperature

½ cup granulated sugar

1 large egg, at room temperature

1 tablespoon finely grated lemon zest

1 teaspoon pure vanilla extract

2 cups all-purpose flour

5 ounces dried currants (about 1 cup)

½ teaspoon baking soda

½ teaspoon kosher salt

Sanding sugar for dipping

Five-Layer Honey Cream Cake

SERVES 10 TO 12

I created this cake after a trip to San Francisco, where the kindest cab driver in the world lent me cash to buy dinner on my way home. No kidding. I was exhausted and hungry after a long photo shoot. My driver heard me rummage through my bag and complain to myself about not having any money to pick up food. Then, she simply said, "I know what that's like," and handed me a twenty.

Then, wouldn't you know, the restaurant I was headed for was closed. But, of course, this being my lucky day, the owner unlocked the doors, welcomed me like an old friend, and gave me my salad to go. It's the same thing every time I go to San Francisco. Someone hands me a new grocery bag after mine rips in the rain. A dressing room companion tells me that the jeans I'm trying on make my butt look good. Those delightful Californians deserve all the cake I can serve up.

And speaking of cake, this one was inspired by the famous Russian Honey Cake served at the 20th Century Café in San Francisco. I indulged more than once on that trip and I created this homey layer cake as my East Coast version. It's rougher around the edges and a bit less refined, but it's sweet and light and much simpler to throw together.

Don't worry if you don't have five 8-inch cake pans. I have only three. Just bake as many layers as you have, pop the baked layers out, clean the pans with cold water to cool them down, and then bake the remaining layers. Use a scale to weigh the batter and divide it evenly. And don't forget to butter the pans and line them with parchment again.

CAKE:

14 tablespoons/1¾ sticks unsalted butter, at room temperature, plus more for pans

⅓ cup mild honey, such as orange blossom

1 teaspoon baking soda

2½ cups all-purpose flour

½ teaspoon baking powder

½ teaspoon kosher salt

¼ teaspoon ground cinnamon

1 cup granulated sugar

2 large eggs

2 large egg yolks

¾ cup whole milk, at room temperature

Prepare the cake: Preheat the oven to 350°F. Butter as many 8-inch cake pans (up to 5) as you have. Line them with parchment paper and butter the parchment.

In a medium saucepan, heat the honey over medium heat just until it becomes runny but before it starts to bubble, about 1 minute. Add the baking soda and stir with a heatproof spatula. The mixture will be foamy and pale. Cook it just until the mixture turns golden, stirring constantly, about 1 minute. Remove the pot from the heat before the mixture takes on a reddish hue. Scrape the honey mixture into a bowl and let cool slightly.

In a medium bowl, whisk together the flour, baking powder, salt, and cinnamon. In a large bowl, beat the butter and granulated sugar with an electric mixer on medium speed until light and fluffy, about 4 minutes. Add the eggs and egg yolks, 1 at a time, scraping the bowl between each addition. Beat in the cooled honey mixture. Reduce the speed to low and alternate adding the flour mixture and the milk, starting and ending with the flour mixture.

HONEY CREAM:

4 ounces cream cheese, at room temperature

¼ cup plus 1 tablespoon honey

1 cup heavy cream, whipped to soft peaks

TO FINISH:

Confectioners' sugar for dusting

Divide the batter evenly among the 5 prepared pans and smooth the tops. Bake until the center of a cake springs back when gently pressed, 10 to 15 minutes. (Don't overbake the layers or they will be dry.) Transfer the pans to a wire rack to cool for 3 minutes, then carefully flip out the cakes.

Prepare the honey cream: Beat the cream cheese and honey until smooth. Fold the whipped cream into the cream cheese mixture.

To assemble, layer the cooled cake layers with the honey cream. Sprinkle with confectioners' sugar to serve.

Glazed Pear Fritters

MAKES 12 FRITTERS

Green and orange turns out to be a color combination that suits me. That was the color of my uniform when I worked in my local doughnut shop, the air hazy with smoke (before the indoor smoking ban). It was my first job, and I loved filling the cream doughnuts with the yellow industrial sludge called "custard." Working the lever on the cream machine to lighten multiple coffee orders at lightning speed took a type of precision that I had in spades. Like a lithe ballerina behind the greasy counter, I spun and sashayed to fill the waxed bags and boxes with treats. My partner in frying was a local chick named Amber who showed me that if you add enough sugar to the iced coffee, it took on a very satisfying crunch and, most important, that stale apple fritters that we would have tossed at the end of the day became satisfyingly gooey with a four-second blast in the microwave. That became our ritual and hard-earned indulgence, a dough happy hour at the end of the day. It wasn't glamorous, but we took pride in the job well done.

These fluffy, yeasty fritters are considerably better than the old ones we ate back then, but the happiness they inspire is the same. I prefer pears to apples, for their yielding texture and floral sweetness. Comice are my favorite for baking, but you could use a few Barletts or some ripe Boscs.

Prepare the dough: Heat the milk in a small saucepan over medium heat just until bubbles form around the edge. Transfer the milk to a small bowl and let it cool to about 110°F. Meanwhile, in a large bowl, whisk together the flour, granulated sugar, yeast, and salt.

Add the egg to the milk and whisk to combine. With a wooden spoon, add the milk mixture to the flour mixture and stir it into a ball. Tip the dough out onto a lightly floured surface and knead the dough until it is smooth, about 5 minutes. You can add a little bit more flour at this point, if necessary.

Next, knead the butter into the dough piece by piece, using a flexible bench scraper to scrape the butter back into the dough as you knead. The dough will seem sticky and buttery, but don't add more flour. Just keep kneading and stretching the dough until the butter is completely absorbed and the dough is smooth. Pop the dough into a buttered bowl, cover tightly with plastic wrap, and refrigerate overnight.

The next day, prepare the pear mixture: Toss the pears with the vinegar in a medium bowl. In a large skillet, melt the butter over medium heat. Sprinkle the granulated sugar over the melted butter and cook, stirring, until the sugar turns deep golden brown, 2 to 3 minutes. (The butter and sugar may separate. Don't worry.) Add the pears and toss to combine.

(continued on next page)

DOUGH:

½ cup whole milk

1¾ cups all-purpose flour, plus more for dusting

2 tablespoons granulated sugar

1¾ teaspoons active dry yeast

½ teaspoon kosher salt

1 large egg

3 tablespoons unsalted butter, at room temperature, plus more for bowl

Vegetable oil for frying

PEAR MIXTURE:

3 small pears, peeled, cored and diced (about 3 cups)

2 teaspoons cider vinegar

2 tablespoons unsalted butter

2 tablespoons granulated sugar

GLAZE:

1 cup confectioners' sugar

1 to 2 tablespoons whole milk

½ teaspoon pure vanilla extract

Cook until the pears release some of their juice and are just tender but still hold their shape, 1 to 2 minutes. Use a slotted spoon to transfer the pears to a plate. Continue to cook the remaining liquid until thick and syrupy, about 3 minutes more. Drizzle the liquid over the pears and toss gently to combine. Let cool to room temperature.

On a lightly floured surface, roll out the chilled dough into a large rectangle about ¼ inch thick, with the short sides at the bottom and the top of the work surface. Use a slotted spoon to transfer half of the pears to cover the bottom half of the rectangle, leaving most of the pear liquid behind on the plate. Fold the top half of the dough over the pear-filled half. Press the dough down to seal in the pears. Spread the rest of the pears, without too much of that liquid, on one side of the dough square. Then, fold the bare half of the dough over the pears and press to seal. Roll this into a ball, transfer it to a buttered bowl, cover lightly with plastic wrap, and set it aside to double, about an hour.

On a floured surface, tip out the risen dough and press it into a big square. Use the bench scraper to cut the dough into 12 equal pieces. Shape each piece into a rough ball as best you can. Don't worry if they seem messy or pears pop out. Just smoosh them back together and proceed. Transfer the pieces to well-floured baking sheets. Cover lightly with plastic wrap and let stand until puffed, about an hour.

Heat 3 inches of oil in a large, heavy-bottomed pot to 360°F. Line a baking sheet with paper towels.

Prepare the glaze: Whisk together the confectioners' sugar, milk, and vanilla in a bowl. Add more milk or a little water, if necessary. The mixture should be runny.

Very carefully transfer a puffed piece of dough to a large spider or spatula and lower it into the oil. Add a few more dough balls, but don't crowd the pan. Cook until they are golden brown and puffed, 2 to 3 minutes, flipping halfway through cooking. Make sure to keep the oil temperature between 350° and 360°F. Lift out the fritters with the spider and set them on the paper towel-lined baking sheet for about 3 minutes, to drain any excess oil.

Transfer the drained fritters to a wire rack and use a pastry brush to cover them with glaze. Serve hot or at room temperature.

Chocolate Cherry Ice Cream

MAKES ABOUT 1 QUART ICE CREAM

Frog and Toad are two amphibian pals who wear blazers and pants and nothing else. They live in a world made up of shades of brown and green, like their own skin, and they look out for each other. I've always appreciated their simple stories of kindness. I hope that my baby boy picks up a thing or two about friendship while we read. In my favorite story, Frog and Toad are craving chocolate ice cream. Frog offers to go to the shop and bring two cones back. On the harrowing journey back, the sun melts the ice cream; it drips all over him. By the time he returns to Frog, Toad looks like a horned chocolate monster. It's only after a frightened tumble into the nearby lake that Frog is relieved to see it's not a monster but his pal. They comfort each other and then return to the store to get the ice cream together. Life doesn't always go as planned, but a good friend can usually make it better. And a bit of chocolate ice cream doesn't hurt one bit.

Prepare the cherries: In a small saucepan, bring the cherries, sugar, and ¾ cup of water to a boil over medium heat. Lower the heat to a simmer and cook until the cherries are tender, about 5 minutes. Remove from the heat, stir in the almond extract, and let the cherries cool in the syrup, then transfer to the fridge to cool completely.

Prepare the ice cream: Set a fine-mesh sieve over a large bowl. Have ready a large bowl of ice water. In a medium bowl, whisk together the egg yolks, cocoa powder, salt, and sugar. In a medium saucepan, bring the cream to a simmer over medium-high heat.

Ladle a bit of the hot cream mixture into the egg yolk mixture and whisk to combine. Continue this process a few times until most of the cream mixture has been whisked into the yolk mixture. Return everything to the saucepan and cook, stirring constantly with a wooden spoon, until it is just thick enough to coat the back of the spoon, 4 to 6 minutes. It's important not to let the mixture come to a boil or it could curdle. Strain this mixture through the sieve. Whisk in the milk. Set the bowl into the larger bowl of ice water. Stir occasionally with a wooden spoon until the mixture is completely chilled and very thick. Alternatively, cover well with plastic wrap and chill in the fridge until very cold, at least 12 hours. Set a metal loaf pan in the freezer to chill.

Strain the cherries out of the syrup. (Save the syrup for cocktails or to pour over plain yogurt or vanilla ice cream.) Freeze the mixture in an ice-cream maker according to the manufacturer's instructions. At the last minute, fold in the chocolate and the cherries. Transfer to the chilled loaf pan, cover tightly with plastic wrap, and freeze until firm, at least 6 hours. Let stand for 5 minutes at room temperature before serving.

CHERRIES:

12 ounces sweet cherries (fresh or frozen but not thawed), pitted (2½ cups)

¾ cup granulated sugar

½ teaspoon almond extract

ICE CREAM:

8 large egg yolks

⅓ cup cocoa powder, Dutch-processed or natural

½ teaspoon kosher salt

1 cup granulated sugar

3 cups heavy cream

1 cup whole milk

4 ounces semisweet chocolate, finely chopped (about 1 cup), chilled

Lemon Cream Cheese Danish Loaf

MAKES 2 LOAVES

A wise friend once told me that "after you have a baby, you eat crow every day." It's true. The number one thing I realize now is how unhelpful I was to my new-parent friends. Specifically when it came to food. I really should have been cranking out the lasagnas. But I didn't really understand. I didn't notice the hunger in their tired eyes. So, I hope with this recipe I can begin to make amends. It makes two loaves with no extra effort. One for you and one for your hungry friend.

If you don't have two loaf pans, you can also use an 8-inch-diameter, 2-inch-deep round cake pan for the second batch. It will bake much faster than the loaf.

DOUGH:

¾ cup warm whole milk (110° to 115°F)

¼ cup granulated sugar, divided

2¼ teaspoons active dry yeast

1 large egg, at room temperature

2 large egg yolks, at room temperature

3 cups all-purpose flour

¾ teaspoon kosher salt

½ cup/1 stick unsalted butter, at room temperature, plus more for bowl and pans

CREAM CHEESE TOPPING:

8 ounces full-fat cream cheese, at room temperature

¼ cup confectioners' sugar

1 large egg, separated

½ teaspoon pure vanilla extract

½ cup Lemon Curd (page 129)

Prepare the dough: In the bowl of a stand mixer, combine the milk, 1 tablespoon of the granulated sugar, and yeast and let stand until foamy, about 5 minutes. With the dough hook running on low speed, add the egg and egg yolks, flour, salt, and the remaining sugar. Continue to mix until a shaggy dough forms, about 3 minutes. Add the butter pieces, a few at a time, and continue to mix the dough until smooth and pliable, 5 to 7 minutes. Alternatively, mix together the ingredients in a large bowl, using a wooden spoon. Knead the dough, in the bowl, until it is shaggy, about 3 minutes. Then, knead in the butter pieces until incorporated. Tip out the dough onto a work surface and continue to knead until smooth. The dough should be supple and smooth and not too sticky.

Remove the dough from the bowl, if you haven't already, butter the bowl, and return the dough. Cover with plastic wrap and let stand at room temperature until doubled, 1 to 2 hours.

Butter two 8½ x 4½-inch loaf pans and line with parchment, leaving a 2-inch overhang on 2 opposite sides. Turn out the dough onto a work surface (you shouldn't need any flour at this point), gently expel the air from it, then pat out the dough and divide in half. Pat each piece into an 8-inch square and roll it into a tight roll. Tuck each roll into a loaf pan, seam-side down. Press the dough into an even layer. Cover with plastic wrap and let stand until doubled in size, about 90 minutes. About 30 minutes before baking, preheat the oven to 375°F.

Meanwhile, make the cream cheese topping: In a medium bowl, combine the cream cheese, confectioners' sugar, egg yolk, and vanilla, reserving the egg white for the next step. Divide the mixture in half and divide between 2 resealable plastic bags. (This makes it easier to spread the mixture over the risen dough without deflating it.)

(continued on page 74)

GLAZE:
¾ cup confectioners' sugar
2 to 4 teaspoons fresh
lemon juice

Just before baking the loaves, carefully brush the some of the egg white on the top of each loaf. Then, snip the corner from 1 of the bags of the cream cheese mixture. Pipe the mixture down the center of each loaf, leaving about a 1-inch bare border on each of the 2 long sides, then spread ¼ cup of the lemon curd down the center of each loaf. It doesn't need to cover the cream cheese mixture completely. (If using a round cake pan for the second loaf, leave a 1-inch bare border around the edge.) Bake the loaves until puffed and set, 35 to 40 minutes. If the cream cheese mixture starts to brown around the edges, cover the loaves with aluminum foil. The internal temperature of the loaves should reach 185°F. Transfer the pans to wire racks to cool for at least 15 minutes. Using the parchment overhang as handles, lift the loaves out of their pans to cool completely.

Prepare the glaze: In a small bowl, whisk together the confectioners' sugar and 2 teaspoons of the lemon juice. Add a little more juice, if necessary, to make a thick glaze. Drizzle the glaze over each loaf.

Pistachio Praline Puffs

MAKES ABOUT 12 PUFFS

When vacationing at a charming inn in the German Alps, you must open your heart to new experiences. Naked coed saunas with the same five couples you see at dinner every night. Supersweet homemade hazelnut schnapps. Mountain biking.

So, years ago, when my now ex-husband asked whether I'd like to rent mountain bikes for a day during a vacation to the German Alps, I gave him an enthusiastic yes. Why not? We'll see more of those electric green hills and snow-capped mountains in one day. We'll get some exercise. We'll have an adventure and support each other when the going gets rough. But it turns out that biking and mountain biking are *not at all* the same thing. Mountain biking is like pushing a compact car *up mountains*. Up and up and up for hours and hours and hours. Across skid-inducing gravel-laden tracks. Through the occasional downpour. Amid schools of mosquitoes that love to feast on sweaty riders whose hands are busy with steering. The day was a misadventure. We did not support each other. We bickered and argued. We stopped snapping only long enough to eat a completely silent lunch of frankfurters and mustard at a pristine antique hunting lodge nestled in a cinematic alpine meadow. The glorious views could do nothing to improve the situation. The next day, we did the same exact trail on foot. Straight uphill on foot for hours is a cakewalk compared to mountain biking.

A cream puff is a synonym for wimp. Perhaps I'm a cream puff. No matter. The praline filling of these puffs is inspired by the famous Paris-Brest, a dessert created to celebrate the old bicycle race that ran Paris to Brest in the late 1800s. I'm going to leave the serious biking to the professionals and stick to serious baking.

Prepare the pastry cream: Bring the milk and cardamom pods to a simmer in a small pot over medium heat. Remove from the heat, cover, and let stand for at least 1 hour or up to overnight. Then, in a medium bowl, whisk together the egg yolks, granulated sugar, cornstarch, and salt. Whisk in the milk until smooth. Return the mixture to the pot and cook it over medium heat, stirring or whisking constantly, until it begins to thicken and comes to a very low boil, 3 to 5 minutes. Let it cook for 1 minute more and then pour it through a fine-mesh sieve set over a medium bowl. Whisk in the butter and vanilla. Press a piece of waxed paper or plastic wrap into the surface of the custard, cover, and refrigerate until cold, at least 2 hours or up to 2 days.

Prepare the praline: Line a rimmed baking sheet with a silicone baking mat. Place 2 tablespoons of water in a small saucepan, then pour the granulated sugar into the center. Heat the sugar mixture over medium heat, (continued on next page)

PASTRY CREAM:
1½ cups whole milk

5 cardamom pods, crushed

5 large egg yolks

2 tablespoons granulated sugar

¼ cup cornstarch

¼ teaspoon kosher salt

1 tablespoon unsalted butter

1 teaspoon pure vanilla extract

¼ cup heavy cream, whipped to stiff peaks

PRALINE:

½ cup granulated sugar

3¾ ounces unsalted raw or roasted pistachios (¾ cup)

CRACKLE DOUGH:

3 tablespoons unsalted butter, at room temperature

¼ cup packed light brown sugar

¼ cup all-purpose flour

¼ teaspoon kosher salt

PUFFS:

1 recipe pâte à choux (page 170)

Confectioners' sugar for sprinkling

swirling the pot occasionally, until it has melted and turned a deep amber color, 6 to 8 minutes. Remove from the heat and immediately stir in the pistachios. Tip out the mixture onto the prepared baking sheet and spread it out into an even layer. Let cool completely.

Once the praline is completely cool, break it into pieces and transfer it to a food processor or blender. Pulse until the mixture has broken down into a fine powder.

Prepare the crackle dough: Beat together the butter, brown sugar, flour, and salt until smooth. Tip out the mixture onto a piece of plastic wrap, form it into a disk, and chill until firm, at least 1 hour.

Prepare the puffs: Preheat the oven to 400°F. Line 2 rimmed baking sheets with parchment paper. Drop the pâte à choux dough in 2-tablespoon scoops about 3 inches apart onto the prepared baking sheets.

On a lightly floured surface, roll out the crackle dough to about ¼-inch thick. Cut twelve 1½-inch circles from the dough, rerolling the scraps as needed. Top each puff with a circle of crackle dough. Bake until deep golden brown and puffed, 22 to 26 minutes, rotating the sheets halfway through baking. Transfer the puffs to a wire rack and let cool completely.

Just before serving, fill the puffs: Fit a piping bag with a ½-inch star tip. Whisk the pastry cream to loosen it and stir in the pistachio praline. Fold in the whipped cream. Fill the pastry bag with the cream mixture. Working from the side or bottom of the puffs, fill each puff with a few tablespoons of the cream mixture. Sprinkle with confectioners' sugar to serve.

Toasted Brown Sugar Crème Caramel

SERVES 6 TO 8

Yo-Yo Ma's cello makes the smoothest sound I've ever heard. The music he plays flows in rich waves that wrap around me like a soft hug. Nothing jars or jabs. I want to melt into his Bach Cello Suites like butter on toast. Close my eyes and lie on them in perfect comfort.

This flan is my interpretation of his sound. Just like his music, the two layers of custard are easy to take in. Burnished to a rich toasted color, like the cello, with the bittersweet notes and creamy texture of the instrument's melancholy voice. Once you've got it in your mouth, you'll realize how surprisingly complex the flavor is. Combining brown sugar and butter and heat, like musical notes, turns simple things toward the sublime.

Preheat the oven to 325°F. Have ready an 8½ x 4½-inch standard loaf pan.

Prepare the caramel: Place 2 tablespoons water in a small saucepan. Add the granulated sugar. Cook the sugar, without stirring, over medium-high heat until it is a deep amber color, about 8 minutes, swirling the pan occasionally to cook evenly. Don't worry if it crystalizes; just keep cooking and swirling. Once it turns amber, it usually softens up again. Immediately pour the caramel into the loaf pan and carefully tip and swirl the pan so that the caramel climbs up all 4 sides as well as covers the bottom. Take care: the caramel is extremely hot; do not let it touch your fingers. Set the pan aside.

Prepare the custard: In a medium saucepan, melt the butter over medium heat. Add the brown sugar and cook, whisking, until the sugar has melted, about 2 minutes. (Don't worry if it seizes a bit. Just make sure the heat isn't too high or the mixture could burn.) Add 1 teaspoon of water and cook, stirring, until the mixture is a deep brown color and smells fragrant and just starts to smoke, another 4 to 5 minutes. Immediately remove the pan from the heat and add ½ cup of the milk. Be careful as it will steam and sputter. Return the pan to very low heat, add the salt, and whisk the mixture until any hard pieces of sugar melt again, about 2 minutes. Transfer the mixture to a large bowl and let cool for a few minutes. Meanwhile, bring a kettle of water to a boil.

Add the remaining 2½ cups of milk, the eggs and egg yolks, and the vanilla and whisk until well combined. (An immersion blender works really well here, but it isn't essential.) Set a fine-mesh sieve over the loaf pan and pour the mixture through. Discard any solids left behind.

Set the loaf pan in a roasting pan. Add boiling water to the roasting pan to come about halfway up around the loaf pan. Cover the loaf pan with foil.

(continued on next page)

CARAMEL:
¾ cup granulated sugar

CUSTARD:
4 tablespoons/½ stick unsalted butter

1 cup packed dark brown sugar

3 cups whole milk, divided

1 teaspoon kosher salt

5 large eggs

3 large egg yolks

1 teaspoon pure vanilla extract

Bake until the custard is set but still jiggles slightly in the center, about 1 hour 15 minutes. Remove from the oven, remove the foil, and let the custard come to room temperature still in the water bath. Lift the pan out of the water, then cover with plastic wrap and transfer to the fridge for at least 4 hours.

To serve, cut around the edges with a thin, sharp knife. Carefully flip the custard onto a rimmed platter or plate.

Roasted Plum Cloud Cake

SERVES 6

This cake is the epitome of living in the moment. With some cakes, you can stir together the batter, throw the pans in the oven, and then use the baking time to give your life a good ponder. Lying on the couch, the aroma of vanilla and sweetness filling your home, you may ask yourself, *Do I need to start researching preschools? Is today the day I should roll those 401(k) accounts into one IRA?* This is not that cake.

While each layer of this dessert bakes, you should be working on the next layer. It's not hard, but it's steady. An opportunity to fully focus on the task at hand. Be present. Be mindful. And keep working. Think of it as baking yoga. In the end, you will be rewarded with a beautiful three-layered beauty. Vanilla-flecked roasted fruit rendered jammy and thick, hugged by a brown-sugar butter cake reminiscent of cobbler with a tender top and fruit-soaked bottom, and topped with a swirly, crisp meringue. It's like a pavlova, flipped on its head with a bit of cake in the middle.

Preheat the oven to 400°F. Place the butter and vanilla bean and seeds in an oven-safe 10-inch skillet. Place the pan in the oven and bake until the butter has melted and browned, about 8 minutes.

Add the sliced plums and brown sugar to the hot butter mixture and toss to coat. Return the pan to the oven and roast until the plums have released their juices and have begun to soften, about 15 minutes. Carefully pluck out the vanilla bean.

Meanwhile, prepare the cake batter: In a small bowl, whisk together the flour, baking powder, baking soda, and salt. In a medium bowl, with an electric mixer on medium speed, beat together the butter and brown sugar until fluffy, about 2 minutes. Beat in the egg yolks, then the flour mixture. Fold in the buttermilk until just combined. Dollop the batter over the plums and spread it out as evenly as you can. Return the pan to the oven and bake the cake for 25 minutes. (At this point it's a good idea to put a rimmed baking sheet on the rack below the cake to catch any plum juices that could drip over the edge.)

Meanwhile, prepare the meringue: In a large bowl, beat the egg whites and cream of tartar with an electric mixer on medium-high speed until they are foamy and lose their yellow hue, about 2 minutes. Then, while beating, add the superfine sugar and beat until you have stiff, shiny peaks, about 9 minutes. Spread the meringue over the cake and bake until the meringue is crisp and light brown, another 25 to 30 minutes. Remove the cake from the oven and let stand for 10 minutes before serving.

PLUM LAYER:

4 tablespoons/½ stick unsalted butter

½ vanilla bean, split and seeds scraped

2 pounds red plums, pitted and cut into ½-inch wedges

2 to 4 tablespoons light brown sugar (depending on the sweetness of the fruit)

CAKE:

1 cup all-purpose flour

½ teaspoon baking powder

¼ teaspoon baking soda

½ teaspoon kosher salt

4 tablespoons/½ stick unsalted butter, at room temperature

¾ cup packed light brown sugar

3 large egg yolks, at room temperature

½ cup buttermilk, at room temperature

MERINGUE:

3 large egg whites

¼ teaspoon cream of tartar

¾ cup superfine sugar

Sunshine Wreath

SERVES 8

The gray skies of New York City tend to linger into April. They blur the lines between those last interminable days of winter and the start of spring. The damp streets. The drab, melancholy buildings. The chill in the air. May is downpour season. Summer is taking too damn long. What to do? Bake a little sunshine before the best citrus is gone.

DOUGH:

⅓ cup warm whole milk (110°F–115°F)

2 teaspoons active dry yeast

¼ cup granulated sugar, divided

2 cups all-purpose flour, plus more for dusting

½ teaspoon kosher salt

1 large egg, at room temperature

1 large egg yolk, at room temperature

4 tablespoons/½ stick unsalted butter, at room temperature

FILLING:

3 tablespoons fresh grated orange zest (from 2 navel oranges)

2 tablespoons freshly grated lemon zest (from 2 large lemons)

6 tablespoons granulated sugar

3 tablespoons unsalted butter, at room temperature

Pinch of salt

TO FINISH:

1 large egg, beaten

Prepare the dough: In a small bowl, combine the milk, yeast, and 1 teaspoon of the sugar. Set aside until foamy, about 5 minutes.

In the bowl of a stand mixer with the dough hook attached, combine the remaining sugar, flour, and salt. With the mixer on low speed, add the yeast mixture, egg, and egg yolk and knead until smooth and elastic, about 5 minutes. Add the butter, a bit at a time, and continue to knead the dough until the butter is fully incorporated and the dough is smooth, another 5 minutes. The dough will be sticky. Scrape down the sides of the bowl and gather the dough into a neat ball. Alternatively, mix together the ingredients in a large bowl, using a wooden spoon. Knead the dough, in the bowl, until it is smooth, about 5 minutes. Then, knead in the butter pieces, a bit at a time, until incorporated. Tip out the dough onto a work surface and continue to knead until smooth but still sticky. Return the dough to the bowl.

Cover with plastic wrap and set aside to rise in a warm place until doubled, 1 to 2 hours. (After the dough has doubled, you can punch it down, wrap it well, and refrigerate for up to 2 days.)

Prepare the filling: In a small bowl, using your fingers, grind the orange zest, lemon zest, and sugar together to release some of the citrus oils. Add the butter and the salt and mix until well combined.

Tip the dough out onto a lightly floured surface. Roll it out into a 17 x 8-inch rectangle. Spread the filling evenly over the surface of the dough. Starting from 1 of the long ends, roll up the dough into a tight coil. Pinch the ends to seal the roll. Using a sharp knife, cut the dough in half lengthwise. Transfer the 2 pieces of dough, cut-side up, to a piece of parchment paper. Pinch the 2 pieces together at 1 end and then carefully twist the 2 pieces of dough together. Take care not to stretch the dough and to keep the cut sides up. Coil the twist around to make a wreath and connect the ends, making sure to continue the twisting pattern. Transfer the wreath, on the parchment, to a rimmed baking sheet. Cover lightly with plastic wrap and set aside in a warm place to rise. It could take up to 2 hours for the wreath to puff, so it's better to keep an eye on the dough rather than on the clock.

Preheat the oven to 375°F. Carefully brush the wreath with the beaten egg. Bake until puffed and golden brown, 25 to 30 minutes. Don't worry if it leaks a bit! It always does. A thermometer inserted into the thickest part of the bread should register between 190° and 200°F. Transfer the pan to a wire rack to cool slightly. Serve warm or at room temperature.

This bread is best the day it's made, but leftovers can be stored in an airtight container at room temperature for up to 2 days or in the freezer for up to 1 month. Warm leftovers before serving.

CHAPTER THREE

BLISS

Following Fairies

I leaned over the pink bathroom sink and stared in sad disbelief. The red sprinkles I had dropped into the warm water floated on the surface, leaching ribbons of red dye. For some reason, they hadn't transformed into a Raggedy Ann doll. Puzzled, I turned to my big brother, Mohan, and asked what happened. "They must not be the right kind." His answer seemed plausible. These weren't the magic sprinkles he had told me about a few nights earlier, the ones that would instantaneously burst into the thing I wanted the most. I lived in a world where my brother knew everything. I pulled the plug and let the defective sprinkles swirl down the drain.

Another day found us heading into the woods looking for more magic. We slathered creamy peanut butter and grape jelly over squishy white bread, wrapped up our sandwiches, and packed them into our backpacks alongside two thermoses of milk. According to Mohan, there was a hidden fairy glen somewhere along the dirt path behind our house that led to the skating pond. Tall golden grass and pussy willows concealed and protected this mythical woodland utopia, but he was sure we could find it if we looked hard enough. I never questioned how he knew about it. I simply closed my eyes and imagined this place where the light sparkled on the water and little doors in the stumps of trees lead to golden tea parties with pretty cakes and iced cookies. I was up for the search. I followed him for hours, swatting tangles of gnats and forging through dried-out brush that knocked me in the face as we passed. When we got hungry, we cleaned off flat rocks and sat by the pond to picnic. At the end of the day, we still hadn't seen even a flicker of a gilded wing. He told me that to keep their home safe, the sprites camouflage it from humans. We probably had walked right past it but never known it. The explanation was even more satisfying than actually seeing anything. Knowing that this world could be anywhere, right next to me but out of sight, filled me with pure delight.

My big brother taught me to believe that the world was filled with magic. After he died, I realized what a gift he had given me. No day was ever mundane with him. A trip to the lighting store could be extraordinary if we imagined a new reality behind the chandeliers. With him, I could spend an entire day sweeping paths and making seating areas through the woods in preparation for an imaginary festival that would never manifest. The preparation *was* the game itself. Because of him, every single dip in our backyard swimming pool commenced with a special blessing dance that made me feel both happy and safe. Life was full of pleasure. Wishes could be granted. Mystical guardians were never far away.

I hope I can create the same magic for my son. He's small now, but when we go on walks through the overgrown paths in the woods of Prospect Park, I hold him close to me and tell him what I know. I tell him what Mohan would have told him if he were here with us now. It's the best way I know to explain to my boy, Arthur Mohan, what a treasure his uncle was. I tell him about the fairies that infuse the roots of the big trees with magic strength so that they can grow big enough to crack through the pavement. I explain how the bushy-tailed squirrels make nougat candy studded with acorns to sell to the chipmunks. And I assure him that on lucky days, the gray pigeons offer to carry our troubles with them to another borough, releasing us from their weight for a little while.

Peppermint Snow Patties

MAKES ABOUT 2 DOZEN PATTIES

Mohan made everything special, even little York Peppermint Patties. As we indulged in our Halloween booty, he told me that the minty white center in each candy was actually snow harvested directly from around Santa's house at the North Pole. Why didn't it melt? Well, it was magic North Pole snow. I stared at the creamy opaque center and wondered whether Santa or Rudolph might have grazed those particular flakes as they walked by on their way to the toy factory. As I chewed, I imagined I saw elves and life-size candy canes.

Believe in magic. Even just for a little while. I promise that your life will be happier for it.

2 cups confectioners' sugar

2 tablespoons Lyle's Golden Syrup

2 tablespoons unsalted butter, at room temperature

½ teaspoon pure peppermint extract

2 to 3 teaspoons heavy cream

12 ounces bittersweet chocolate, coarsely chopped (about 3 cups)

In a large bowl with an electric mixer on medium speed, beat the confectioners' sugar, golden syrup, and butter until well combined, about 3 minutes. Add the peppermint extract and 2 teaspoons of the cream and beat until a stiff dough has formed. Add up to 1 more teaspoon of cream, if necessary. Tip out the dough onto a piece of plastic wrap and roll it out to ¼ inch thick. Wrap well and freeze for 20 minutes.

Line a rimmed baking sheet with parchment. Using a 1½-inch round cookie cutter, cut circles from the dough and transfer them to the prepared pan. Reroll the scraps on the plastic wrap as necessary.

Melt the chocolate over a double boiler or in short bursts in the microwave. Using 2 forks, dip each peppermint round into the chocolate, tap off the excess, and place on the prepared baking sheet. Chill until firm.

Store the candies in an airtight container in the fridge for up to 2 weeks. Let them come to room temperature before serving.

BASIC

I have a tattoo on my foot. I cringe when anyone notices it and I have to explain. When my mom first saw it in 1998, she thought it was black dirt that had kicked up onto my foot from walking around the city in flip-flops.

It's small, thank goodness, about 2 inches on the inner part of my right foot, just below the ankle. The script is my mother's handwriting. It says *satuta*, which means "joy" in Sinhalese. I asked her to write the word on a piece of paper so I that had something to take to the tattoo parlor. She never questioned me. The dark black ink has faded into an ugly navy blue. The letters have lost their definition so that instead of a word, it looks more like a hairy caterpillar looking for a leaf.

It took me a few years to realize how deeply unoriginal it is to have the word *joy* etched into your skin for eternity. I think this is exactly what the kids these days would deem "basic." At the very least, I know my tattoo means what I think it means—always a risk of getting one in a language you don't actually speak. Remember Ariana Grande's Japanese "tiny barbecue grill" tattoo? She handled it well, poor thing.

And sometimes I can think back twenty years and feel a softness for my younger self. Some college kids have a plan. I had dozens. I worked through a whole smorgasbord of unrelated classes from Organismal Biology to Geography of Our National Parks to Music of the World and back to Principles of Economics. Way back in 1998, I had a hunch that the Internet with a capital "I" was going to be big, so I even suffered through a computer science class to learn basic coding. (By the end of the semester I had created a static webpage with a white grid on it. Money well spent.)

I wasn't quite certain who I wanted to be, but I knew what I wanted above all. I wanted to be happy. I thought that if maybe I stamped the word onto my body, the undeniable fact of it would stay with me. I would literally always have joy, no matter what were to happen in the rest of my life. They say that forcing a smile, even a fake smile, sends a signal to the brain and makes you a smidge happier. I designed a tattoo to be my permanent fake smile.

Merriam-Webster, not to be confused with the Urban Dictionary, defines the adjective *basic* as "forming the base or essence." That is pretty much exactly what I hoped to accomplish. And to be honest, it kind of works.

Thanks, Chronic Tattoo of Elyria, Ohio. I don't regret one bit the twenty minutes and forty dollars I spent with you. In fact, I like the work you did on me so much that I named a book after it.

Chocolate Almond Spelt Shortbread

MAKES 35 COOKIES

Classic shortbread is the most basic of all the cookies but I've never been one to leave well enough alone. With the addition of spelt flour, brown sugar, chocolate, and almonds, there's more to these guys than meets the eye.

Preheat the oven to 325°F. Butter a 13 x 9-inch baking pan. Line the pan with parchment, leaving a 2-inch overhang on 2 opposite sides. Butter the parchment.

In a medium bowl, whisk together the spelt flour, all-purpose flour, cornstarch, and salt. In a large bowl, with an electric mixer on medium speed, beat the butter, brown sugar, and confectioners' sugar until just smooth, about 2 minutes. Beat in the vanilla. Add the flour mixture and beat until the mixture is evenly moistened and resembles clumpy sand. (Stop before you've got a uniformly creamy dough.) Beat in the chocolate and almonds.

Transfer the mixture to the prepared pan. Using the bottom of a lightly floured dry measuring cup, press the crumbs into an even layer. Using a bench scraper or sharp knife, cut the bars all the way through into 35 rectangles (7 by 5). Sprinkle evenly with the sanding sugar.

Bake until deep golden brown and dry, 45 to 55 minutes. Remove from the oven and, while the bars are still warm, use a sharp knife to recut the bars. You can use a fork to make a decorative pattern in each cookie if you like. Transfer the pan to a wire rack to cool completely.

Use the parchment overhang as handles to lift the bars out of the pan and recut as necessary.

Keep the shortbread in an airtight container up to 1 week or in the freezer for up to 1 month.

1½ cups/3 sticks unsalted butter, at room temperature but not too soft, plus more for pan

2¼ cups spelt flour

1 cup all-purpose flour, plus more for dusting

3 tablespoons cornstarch

1¼ teaspoons kosher salt

⅔ cup packed dark brown sugar

½ cup confectioners' sugar

2 teaspoons pure vanilla extract

3 ounces bittersweet or semisweet chocolate, chopped (about ¾ cup)

3 ounces sliced almonds, chopped (¾ cup)

Sanding sugar for sprinkling

Neapolitan Ice-Cream Cake

SERVES 8 TO 10

I hate to admit it, but I was the problem child at every birthday party. My problem, specifically, was that I was antipizza and anticake. What the heck was my issue? Happily, there was another birthday party staple that I loved. Neapolitan ice cream in a white paper cup. Naples doesn't get enough credit for these beauties. I loved pulling the very small tab and folding back the flimsy white top to expose three beautiful colors, milky pale and perfect. Tucking in with a flat wooden stick that occasionally became sort of dangerous to put in your mouth. Each bite had to have a little bit of each flavor. If you can get your hands on a twelve-pack of these little guys, I will happily attend your party.

Fresh Strawberries and Cream Ice Cream (page 157) is perfect, especially in the summer when strawberries are abundant and flavorful, but feel free to use your favorite store-bought variety in a pinch.

CAKE:
½ cup/1 stick unsalted butter, plus more for pan

1¾ cups cake flour

1¾ teaspoons baking powder

¾ teaspoon kosher salt

¾ cup whole milk

3 large eggs, at room temperature

2 large egg yolks, at room temperature

1 cup granulated sugar

1½ teaspoons pure vanilla extract

CHOCOLATE LAYER:
4½ ounces semisweet chocolate, chopped (1 cup)

2 tablespoons coconut oil

ICE-CREAM LAYER:
1 recipe Strawberries and Cream Ice Cream (page 157; see note)

FROSTING:
¾ cup confectioners' sugar

½ cup cocoa powder, Dutch-processed or natural

Prepare the cake: Preheat the oven to 325°F. Butter a 9-inch-diameter, 2-inch-deep round cake pan and line with parchment paper.

In a medium bowl, whisk together the cake flour, baking powder, and salt. In a small saucepan, heat the butter and milk to a simmer over medium heat, just until the butter has melted. Remove the pot from the heat and let cool slightly.

In a large bowl, with an electric mixer on high speed, beat the eggs, egg yolks, and granulated sugar until thick and pale, about 5 minutes. (The mixture should be able to hold a ribbon.) Beat in the milk mixture on low speed. Then, beat in the flour mixture. Beat in the vanilla. Transfer the batter to the prepared pan and bake until the cake springs back in the center when gently pressed and a toothpick inserted into the center comes out with moist crumbs, 45 to 55 minutes. Transfer the pan to a wire rack to cool for 15 minutes. Use a sharp knife to release the cake from the pan around the edges and flip it out onto a wire rack to cool completely. Remove and discard the parchment paper.

Prepare the chocolate layer: Melt the chocolate and coconut oil together in short bursts in the microwave or in a double boiler on the stovetop. Whisk until smooth.

Assemble the cake: Cut the cake horizontally into 2 even layers. Set 1 layer on a platter, cut-side up. Spread half of the chocolate mixture evenly over the top of the cake layer, leaving a neat 1-inch bare border around the edge. Set the frozen disk of ice cream on top of the cake layer. Spread the remaining chocolate evenly over the cut side of the remaining cake layer, then place it on top of the ice-cream layer, cut-side (chocolate-side) down. Wrap the cake in plastic wrap and freeze for 10 minutes, while you prepare the frosting.

(continued on page 92)

Large pinch of kosher salt

⅓ cup whole milk

1¾ cups cold heavy cream

1 teaspoon pure vanilla extract

Prepare the frosting: In a large bowl, whisk together the confectioners' sugar, cocoa powder, and salt. Whisk in the milk until you have a smooth paste. Add the cream and vanilla beat with an electric mixer on high speed until stiff peaks form, about 3 minutes. You can hold the frosting in the fridge for up to 24 hours before assembling the cake.

To serve, spread the frosting evenly over the cake.

This cake is best eaten immediately so that the cake layer and the frosting are soft while the ice cream is firm. You can store any leftovers, well wrapped, in the freezer.

Note: Instead of freezing the ice cream in a metal loaf pan as the recipe on page 157 suggests, freeze it in a plastic wrap–lined 9-inch round cake pan. When it comes time to assemble the cake, simply lift out the round and place it in the cake.

Brownie Cake with Candied Hazelnuts and Whipped Cream

SERVES 8

At five a.m., his room has the blue-gray cast of night with only the hint of sunrise orange. I roll out of bed when I hear him start to babble and whinny and make my way to the nursery. It's earlier than I would otherwise leave the fluffy rolls of my bed, but I do it without hesitation. When I stumble into his room, he is deeply and wholly happy to see me. There isn't an ounce of judgment, worry, or complaint concealed behind his smile. There are no hidden feelings. He brings his chubby hands to his mouth. He squeezes his cheeks into a smile so wide that his gigantic eyes practically disappear, he kicks his legs up over his head, and he squeals with delight.

Every morning with my son is like a brownie cake. No matter how many brownies you've eaten before, the sight of new ones always elicits glee: Oh! I remember you! You're back, and I'm so happy.

CAKE:

¾ cup/1½ sticks unsalted butter, melted, plus more for pan

1 cup granulated sugar

¾ cup dark brown sugar

¼ cup vegetable oil

4 large eggs

2 teaspoons pure vanilla extract

¾ cup cocoa powder

1 cup all-purpose flour

½ cup hazelnut meal

¾ teaspoon kosher salt

¾ teaspoon ground cinnamon

½ teaspoon instant espresso powder

¼ teaspoon baking powder

CANDIED HAZELNUTS:

⅓ cup granulated sugar

½ teaspoon salt

2¼ ounces hazelnuts, toasted and skinned (½ cup)

TO FINISH:

2 cups whipped cream

Prepare the cake: Preheat the oven to 350°F. Butter an 9-inch round cake pan and line the bottom with parchment. In a medium heavy-bottomed pot, melt the butter over medium heat. Turn off the heat and add the granulated sugar and the brown sugar and stir the mixture for about 90 seconds. Stir in the oil, eggs, and vanilla until smooth. Stir in the cocoa powder, flour, hazelnut meal, salt, cinnamon, espresso powder, and baking powder until well combined. Transfer the batter to the prepared pan. Bake until a toothpick inserted into the center comes out with very moist crumbs attached, 34 to 38 minute. Do not overbake. Transfer to a rack to cool completely.

Prepare the candied hazelnuts: Line a rimmed baking sheet with a silicone baking mat. Place 2 tablespoons of water in a small saucepan. Add the granulated sugar and salt to the center of the pan. Bring the mixture to a simmer over medium heat, carefully swirling the pan (but not stirring with any other tools) until it is a golden amber color, 6 to 8 minutes. Immediately remove the pan from the heat and stir in the hazelnuts. Tip out the mixture onto the prepared pan and press it into an even layer. Let cool completely, then chop finely.

To serve, cut around the edge of the cake pan with a knife, then carefully flip out the cake onto a wire rack. Flip the cake back over onto a serving plate. Top with the whipped cream and sprinkle with the candied hazelnuts.

Cannoli Cream Puffs

MAKES ABOUT 12

The best way to eat a cannoli is standing on the street just outside the pasticceria from which it came. On a sunny April afternoon. In Italy. Trust me. Today, I'm giving you a recipe for these cannoli cream puffs. Choux pastry may not be Italian, but it's quicker and easier than making cannoli shells. I ate these on the fire escape of my Brooklyn apartment on a sunny day in May: a suitable approximation.

I have never loved the flavor of store-bought candied orange peel, a classic garnish for Sicilian cannoli. I've found that a bit of grated orange zest and some chewy dried apricots folded into the cream make a delicious alternative.

1 recipe pâte à choux (page 170)

1½ cups ricotta cheese

½ cup confectioners' sugar, plus more for dusting

1½ teaspoons finely grated orange zest

½ teaspoon ground cinnamon

2 teaspoons pure vanilla extract

3 ounces semisweet chocolate, chopped (about ¾ cup)

1½ ounces dried apricots, minced (¼ cup)

½ cup cold heavy cream

Preheat the oven to 400°F. Line 2 rimmed baking sheets with parchment paper. Drop the pâte à choux dough in 2-tablespoon scoops about 3 inches apart onto the prepared sheets. Bake until deep golden brown and puffed, 22 to 26 minutes, rotating the sheets halfway through baking. Transfer the puffs to a wire rack and let cool completely.

Meanwhile, prepare the filling: In a food processor, process the ricotta, confectioners' sugar, orange zest, cinnamon, and vanilla until smooth. Transfer to a bowl. Stir in the chocolate and apricots.

In a medium bowl, with an electric mixer on medium speed or by hand with a balloon whisk, beat the cream until you have stiff peaks. Fold the cream into the ricotta mixture.

To serve, cut the top third of each puff with a serrated knife. Remove some of the eggy center, if you like. (This makes a delicious cook's treat!) Divide the filling evenly among the puffs and replace the tops. Dust with confectioners' sugar to serve.

Walnut Cake with Penuche Fudge Frosting for Dad

SERVES 8 TO 10

My favorite of the several sarongs my father wore around the house had wide horizontal stripes in several shades of maroon. When my father sat down, he made sure to scoot to the edge of his seat so that his sarong dipped down between his knees and made a small me-size hammock. I referred to this spot as his yap. Not a lap exactly, but a cloth hammock made even cozier by the two armrests of his legs. I just had to waddle over and ask, "Can I sit in your yap?" and he made a space for me.

My dad has a proclivity for sweetness, in children and desserts both. This penuche fudge frosting, intensely sweet and creamy, is not for the faint of heart. I love it slathered all over a humble walnut cake. A little nibble goes a long way. Unless you are my sweetest dad, who can never get enough.

Preheat the oven to 350°F. Butter a 9-inch round springform pan.

Prepare the cake: In a medium bowl, whisk together the flour, baking powder, cinnamon, salt, and baking soda. In a large bowl, using an electric mixer, beat the butter and granulated sugar on medium speed until pale and fluffy, about 3 minutes. Add the eggs, 1 at a time, scraping down the bowl as necessary. Beat in the vanilla.

Add half of the flour mixture and beat on low speed to combine. Beat in the buttermilk. Then, add the remaining flour mixture and walnuts and beat just until combined. Transfer the batter to the prepared pan and smooth the top.

Bake until the cake is set and a toothpick inserted into the center comes out with moist crumbs attached, 40 to 45 minutes. Transfer the pan to a wire rack to cool completely.

Prepare the frosting: In a saucepan, stir together the brown sugar, ⅓ cup of the cream, and the maple syrup, butter, and salt. Bring the mixture to a low boil over medium-low heat. Continue to cook the mixture, without stirring, until thick and dark, about 8 minutes. Transfer to a large bowl and let stand at room temperature to cool for 10 minutes. Add the confectioners' sugar and vanilla and beat with an electric mixer on medium speed until combined. Add the remaining 2 tablespoons of cream and beat the frosting until it is smooth and creamy and thick enough to spread on the cake, 2 to 3 minutes. The cooler the frosting gets, the stiffer it will become, so don't beat it for too long. Tip the cooled cake onto a serving plate and frost with the prepared frosting. Let cool to room temperature to serve.

CAKE:

½ cup/1 stick unsalted butter, at room temperature, plus more for pan

2 cups all-purpose flour, plus more for dusting

1½ teaspoon baking powder

1 teaspoon ground cinnamon

¾ teaspoon kosher salt

¼ teaspoon baking soda

1 cup granulated sugar

2 large eggs

1½ teaspoons pure vanilla extract

¾ cup buttermilk

1 cup walnuts, finely chopped (about 4 ounces)

FROSTING:

1 cup packed dark brown sugar

⅓ cup plus 2 tablespoons heavy cream, divided

2 tablespoons pure maple syrup

4 tablespoons/½ stick unsalted butter

¾ teaspoon salt

1 cup confectioners' sugar

1 teaspoon pure vanilla extract

Coconut Buns

MAKES 18 SMALL BUNS

During my son's first days in the world, I learned about a baby's rooting reflex. Hungry babies will move their little face around, searching for a food source. Graze their soft little cheek or gently touch your finger to their lips and they may open their mouth and search silently, nuzzling their tiny face into your chest, looking for the goods. I can't imagine anything sweeter. In a perfect world, we'd all have the opportunity to just close our eyes, move our face around, and be greeted by something delicious. I definitely wouldn't object to finding a pillowy coconut bun in front of me right now. Close your eyes and enjoy.

If your coconut has a coarse shred, measure it by weight for more accuracy.

DOUGH:

2 teaspoons active dry yeast

¼ cup granulated sugar, divided

½ cup coconut milk, warmed to 105° to 110°F

2 cups all-purpose flour, plus more for dusting

½ teaspoon kosher salt

1 large egg, at room temperature

¼ cup melted coconut oil, plus more for baking dish

FILLING:

1 cup finely shredded unsweetened desiccated coconut (about 3 ounces)

¼ cup Lyle's Golden Syrup

1 large egg yolk

4 tablespoons/½ stick unsalted butter, melted

¼ teaspoon kosher salt

TO FINISH:

1 large egg, lightly beaten

2 tablespoons Lyle's Golden Syrup

1 to 2 teaspoons warm water

Prepare the dough: Stir the yeast and 1 teaspoon of the sugar into the coconut milk. Set aside until foamy, about 5 minutes. Meanwhile, in the bowl of a stand mixer with the dough hook attached, combine the remaining sugar, flour, and salt. With the mixer on low speed, add the yeast mixture, egg, and coconut oil and knead until smooth and elastic, 5 to 10 minutes. The dough will be sticky. Scrape down the sides of the bowl and gather the dough into a neat ball. Alternatively, mix together the sugar, flour, and salt in a large bowl, using a wooden spoon. Add the yeast mixture, egg, and coconut oil and knead until incorporated. Tip out the dough onto a work surface and continue to knead until smooth but still sticky. Return the dough to the bowl.

Cover with plastic wrap and set aside to rise in a warm place until doubled, 1 to 2 hours. (After the dough has doubled, you can punch it down, wrap it well, and refrigerate for up to 2 days.)

Prepare the filling: In a food processor, combine the coconut, golden syrup, egg yolk, butter, and salt and process until finely ground and well combined, scraping down the bowl as necessary. Transfer to a bowl, cover, and set aside.

Oil a 2-quart oval baking dish with melted coconut oil. Tip the dough out onto a lightly floured work surface and knead it a few times to expel the air. Divide it into 18 equal pieces. Roll each piece into a ball. Working with 1 ball at a time, use your thumbs to make a space in the center, add a heaping teaspoon of the filling, and then pinch the seam closed. Roll the filled dough back into a tight ball and place in the prepared dish. Cover and set aside to puff, about 1 hour. After about 40 minutes, preheat the oven to 350°F.

When the balls are puffed and touching one another, carefully brush them with the beaten egg. Bake until golden brown and set, even in the center, about 25 minutes. Combine the golden syrup and water and brush evenly over the warm buns. Serve warm or at room temperature.

Dark Chocolate Malt Celebration Cake

SERVES 10 TO 12

I sat cross-legged on the carpeted floor of my rented canalhouse apartment in Amsterdam, hunched over my neatly packed suitcase. Every item had appeared to be in its place, perfectly rolled and folded. And then I saw a rogue sprinkle. I gingerly plucked the offending confection off my shirt, careful not to streak the fabric with chocolate, and popped it into my mouth. No sense in wasting a good sprinkle.

I dug a little deeper. I found a pocket of four more and ate them one by one. Then another little reservoir. Then another. The box of dark chocolate De Ruijter sprinkles that I had planned to cart back to the States had sprung a tiny leak. Little pockets of sprinkles were sprinkled in every pocket of my suitcase. As I tracked them through my luggage, I imagined myself a contented chimpanzee at mealtime, carefully digging for ants. I searched with deliberate intensity for precious sustenance that I discovered only in tiny but triumphant increments. Try it in your kitchen after you decorate this cake.

To evenly apply sprinkles onto a frosted cake, place the cake on a cake stand set in a rimmed baking sheet. Pour the sprinkles into your hand, aim at the cake, and blow gently. Make a wish. Rotate and repeat.

This cake is killer the next day, zapped for a few seconds in the microwave and served with a big glass of milk. (Eat while wearing pajamas, either for breakfast or a midnight snack.)

Prepare the cake: Preheat the oven to 350°F. Butter two 9-inch round cake pans and line with parchment. Butter the parchment.

In a large bowl, whisk together the cocoa powder and the boiling water until smooth. Add the sour cream and coffee. Add the oil, eggs, and brown sugar and whisk until smooth. In a medium bowl, whisk together the flour, malted milk powder, baking powder, baking soda, and salt. Fold the dry ingredients into the wet ingredients.

Divide the batter between the prepared pans and bake until a toothpick inserted into the center comes out with moist crumbs attached, 35 to 40 minutes. Transfer the pans to a wire rack to cool slightly. Remove the cakes from the pans and transfer to the rack to cool completely.

Prepare the frosting: In a small saucepan, whisk together the cream and malted milk powder and bring to a simmer over medium-high heat. Place the chocolate in a heatproof bowl. Pour the cream mixture over chocolate and let stand for 1 minute. Whisk the chocolate mixture until smooth. Whisk in the butter and salt.

Let the frosting stand at room temperature until smooth and spreadable, stirring occasionally, about 1 hour.

(continued on next page)

CAKE:

Unsalted butter for pans

1¼ cups unsweetened, Dutch-processed cocoa powder

¾ cup boiling water

¾ cup sour cream

½ cup brewed coffee, cooled slightly

¾ cup vegetable oil

3 large eggs

1¼ cups packed dark brown sugar

2 cups all-purpose flour

1½ cups plain malted milk powder

2 teaspoons baking powder

½ teaspoon baking soda

¾ teaspoon kosher salt

FROSTING:

1½ cups heavy cream

1 cup plain malted milk powder

12 ounces semisweet chocolate, chopped (about 3 cups)

1 tablespoon unsalted butter

Pinch of salt

Sprinkles, for extra fun

Trim the cakes so that they are flat. Transfer a cake layer to a serving plate, trimmed-side up. Top with about 1 cup of frosting. Top with the second cake layer, flat-side up, and cover the cake with the remaining frosting. Sprinkle liberally with sprinkles.

Frozen Lime Pie

SERVES 8 TO 10

The pucker-inducing lime filling in this pie is a classic semifreddo. Feel free to tip that mixture into a plastic-wrap lined loaf pan, freeze it, and dig in by the spoonful when you want. If you feel like going the extra mile, the graham cracker crust and toasted meringue topping give this pie summertime flare. A backyard barbecue is always more fun when there's a blowtorch.

Prepare the crust: Preheat the oven to 350°F. In a standard 9-inch pie plate, toss the crumbs, sugar, salt, and melted butter together with a fork. Using a flat-bottomed measuring cup, press the crumbs evenly onto the bottom and sides of the pan. Set the pan on a rimmed baking sheet for easier handling and transfer to the oven. Bake until the crust is lightly browned and fragrant, about 10 minutes. Transfer the pan to a wire rack to cool completely.

Prepare the filling: In a large bowl, with an electric mixer on medium speed, whip the cream to soft peaks and transfer to the refrigerator. In the bowl of a stand mixer, combine the egg yolks, lime zest and juice, sugar, and salt. Set the bowl over a small pot of barely simmering water, making sure the bottom of the bowl isn't touching the water. Whisk the mixture constantly until the sugar is completely dissolved and it has reached 170°F, 4 to 6 minutes. Transfer the bowl to the mixer, fitted with the whisk attachment, and whisk the mixture until it becomes pale, thick, very fluffy, and completely cool, about 10 minutes. (Test the temperature by feeling the underside of the bowl.) Add the whipped cream to the lime mixture and fold them gently to combine. Transfer the mixture to the prepared crust and gently smooth it out. Cover lightly with plastic wrap and freeze until firm, at least 6 hours.

Just before serving, prepare the meringue topping: In the bowl of a stand mixer fitted with a clean whisk attachment, or in a large bowl, using an electric mixer, beat the egg whites and cream of tartar on medium speed until the yellow hue has disappeared and the whites are foamy, 1 to 2 minutes. With the mixer running, gradually add the sugar. Increase the speed to high and beat until the whites are glossy and forms stiff peaks, 4 to 6 minutes. Stop the mixer and feel the meringue with your fingers. You shouldn't be able to feel any grains of sugar. Whisk in the vanilla.

Dollop the top of the pie with the meringue. Using a kitchen torch held a few inches away from the meringue, quickly and evenly brown it. Take care not to apply heat to the frozen pie. Serve immediately. Store leftovers in the freezer.

CRUST:

6 ounces graham crackers, crushed to crumbs (2 cups)

2 tablespoons granulated sugar

¼ teaspoon kosher salt

5 tablespoons unsalted butter, melted

FILLING:

1 cup cold heavy cream

4 large egg yolks (reserve the whites for the topping)

2 tablespoons finely grated lime zest (from 4 limes)

½ cup fresh lime juice (from 4 limes)

½ cup granulated sugar

¼ teaspoon kosher salt

MERINGUE TOPPING:

4 large egg whites, at room temperature

Pinch of cream of tartar

1 cup granulated sugar

¼ teaspoon pure vanilla extract

Gingered Cashew Nut Brittle

MAKES ABOUT 24 SERVINGS

The perfect crackle of a loaf of bread when it comes out of the oven. The smooth grinding of sugar into butter that sends chills up my spine. The soft thud of a knife gliding through cake and gently tapping the plate. Everyone talks about the tastes and smells, but the sounds of baking are just luscious, if you ask me. Certainly the pleasure of a good brittle is as much about the sound as it is about the taste. Cracking it into pieces yields a glassy clatter from the sugar, with the buttery nuts adding a bass-note thud. A brittle-sweet symphony, that's life.

1 tablespoon unsalted butter, plus more for pan

1¼ cups granulated sugar

½ cup Lyle's Golden Syrup

1 teaspoon kosher salt

10½ ounces roasted, salted cashews (2 cups)

¼ cup sesame seeds

3 tablespoons minced, crystallized ginger

1½ teaspoons pure vanilla extract

1 teaspoon baking soda

Butter a 13 x 9-inch rimmed baking sheet or baking pan. In a medium, heavy-bottomed saucepan, combine the butter, sugar, golden syrup, salt, and ½ cup of water. Using a pastry brush dipped in water, brush the sides of the pan to make sure all the grains of sugar have been washed down. Attach a candy thermometer to the side of the pan, making sure the tip of the thermometer is submerged in the mixture.

Because you'll need to work quickly, have ready the cashews, sesame seeds, ginger, vanilla, and baking soda, as well as a wooden spoon and a buttered offset spatula. Heat the sugar mixture over medium-high heat until the temperature reaches 305° to 310°F, 12 to 14 minutes. Add the cashews, sesame seeds, ginger, and vanilla and stir with the wooden spoon to combine. (Make sure the ginger pieces are dispersed evenly.)

Remove the pan from the heat and immediately stir in the baking soda. Be careful; it will foam up and sputter. Transfer the mixture to the prepared pan and quickly spread it evenly with the prepared spatula. Take care not to deflate it. Set aside until completely cool, about 1 hour.

Using the offset spatula, lift out the brittle onto a work surface and crack into pieces. Store in an airtight container at room temperature for up to 1 week.

Graham Cupcakes with Milk Chocolate Frosting

MAKES 12 CUPCAKES

What is bliss if not a little girl, in her favorite cherry red dress, opening the door to greet the guests to her fifth birthday party? When the party was over and the clown had finished tying his last balloon animal and the cake had been devoured, my brother decided to interview me. We sat on the rec room floor, tape recorder poised and ready, and talked about the day. "What do you want to be when you grow up?" "A baker and a librarian." "A baker and a librarian?" He was incredulous. "Well, I might just change my mind, and I'll just be a baker. And I just did. Just now." And so it is.

These are the kind of cupcakes I would bake for my birthday party now. The sweetness of the glossy milk chocolate frosting is mitigated by the nutty graham flour and the addition of honey and molasses give them a delicious gingerbread essence.

Prepare the cake: Preheat the oven to 350°F. Line a standard 12-well muffin tin with paper liners.

In a medium bowl, whisk together the graham flour, cake flour, baking powder, cinnamon, and salt. In a large bowl, whisk together the butter, brown sugar, honey, molasses, eggs, vanilla, and sour cream. Fold the dry ingredients into the wet ingredients.

Divide the batter evenly among the prepared wells and bake until a toothpick inserted into the center of a cupcake comes out with moist crumbs, 16 to 20 minutes. Transfer the cupcakes to a wire rack to cool completely.

Prepare the frosting: Melt the chocolate and butter in short bursts in the microwave or in a double boiler on the stovetop. Let cool to room temperature. Then, stir in the sour cream, vanilla, and salt. Add confectioners' sugar to taste. Spread evenly over the tops of the cooled cakes.

CAKE:

1 cup graham flour

1 cup cake flour

2 teaspoons baking powder

1½ teaspoons ground cinnamon

½ teaspoon kosher salt

½ cup/1 stick unsalted butter, melted

½ cup packed dark brown sugar

¼ cup honey

⅓ cup molasses

2 large eggs

2 teaspoons pure vanilla extract

½ cup full-fat sour cream

FROSTING:

6 ounces good-quality milk chocolate, chopped (about 1½ cups)

2 tablespoons unsalted butter, at room temperature

¾ cup full-fat sour cream

½ teaspoon pure vanilla extract

½ teaspoon kosher salt

1 to 2 tablespoons confectioners' sugar, to taste

Guava Cream Cheese Rugelach

MAKES 2 DOZEN COOKIES

Soft sand, blue water, permanent sun, cool breeze: a spontaneous mid-March trip to Miami from dreary-as-hell New York City. Peel off the sweaters and the socks. Throw on a bikini and a floppy hat. The sun toasts shoulders that haven't felt warmth in months. I'm drunk with the pleasure of heat. Sunburn or bust.

I stole away this year for a weekend of tropical bliss with three friends. When we got back, I made rugelach inspired by the flaky guava pastries we ate in between our morning beach session and afternoon pool hang.

The texture of guava paste varies depending on the brand. You may need more or less water to soften the guava paste. It should be the texture of a very thick, spreadable jam.

DOUGH:

½ cup/1 stick unsalted butter, at room temperature

4 ounces cream cheese, at room temperature

¼ cup granulated sugar

Seeds scraped from ½ vanilla bean

½ teaspoon kosher salt

1 cup all-purpose flour, plus more for dusting

GUAVA FILLING:

5 ounces guava paste, diced

CREAM CHEESE FILLING:

4 ounces cream cheese, at room temperature

¼ cup confectioners' sugar

TO FINISH:

¼ cup plus 2 tablespoons unsweetened finely shredded coconut

1 large egg, lightly beaten

Prepare the dough: In a large bowl, with an electric mixer on medium speed, beat the butter, cream cheese, granulated sugar, vanilla bean seeds, and salt until fluffy, about 2 minutes. Add the flour and beat until evenly moistened. Tip out the dough onto a piece of plastic wrap and bring it together. Divide the dough in half. Wrap each half with plastic wrap and shape into a disk. Chill for at least 2 hours or up to 3 days (alternatively, you can freeze the dough for up to 1 month).

Prepare the guava filling: In a small saucepan, heat the guava paste over medium-low heat with 2 to 3 tablespoons of water, as needed, smashing it occasionally, until it is smooth and jam-like but not too thin, 3 to 5 minutes. Remove from the heat and set aside to cool completely.

Prepare the cream cheese filling: In a small bowl, combine the cream cheese and confectioners' sugar.

On a lightly floured surface, roll out 1 disk of dough to an 11-inch circle. (If at any point the dough becomes too soft, you can transfer it to a parchment-lined baking sheet and pop it into the fridge for a few minutes.) Spread half of the cream cheese mixture on the top of the dough, leaving a ¼-inch bare border. Top with half of the guava mixture, and sprinkle with half of the coconut. With a pizza wheel or sharp knife, cut the dough into 12 equal triangles. Starting from the wide end, roll up each triangle. Place at least 1 inch apart on a parchment-lined rimmed baking sheet. Chill the cookies for 15 minutes. Repeat with the remaining dough, cream cheese mixture, guava mixture, and coconut and transfer to another prepared sheet. Chill.

Preheat the oven to 375°F. Brush each cookie with the beaten egg and bake until they are puffed and golden brown, 20 to 25 minutes, rotating the sheets once. Transfer the baking sheets to a wire rack to cool.

Honey Nut Coffee Cake

SERVES 8 TO 10

New York City stinks. Garbage, exhaust, crowds of human beings, and who really knows what. Fortunately there are little pockets of fragrance everywhere. My favorite city smell comes from the street-nut carts. The men who mind the carts stand all day long tossing peanuts in sugar over heat in copper drums, sending burnished sugar smoke wafting down the sidewalk. There's no need to advertise or call out for customers. That smell, on an early fall afternoon, half hot and half cool, is like a magnet.

This candied–peanut butter cake is an ode to those nut-cart guys. Thank you for making New York a little more wonderful.

Add 2 cups of raspberries to the cake if you'd like a peanut butter and jelly effect, or keep it plain for simple butter-nut bliss.

Prepare the topping: In a small saucepan, combine the butter, sugar, honey, and cream. Heat the mixture over medium heat until the butter is melted, stirring occasionally. Bring the mixture to a boil over medium heat, until a bit lighter in color, about 3 minutes. Add the peanuts and cook until the caramel thickens slightly, 1 minute more. Transfer to a bowl and let cool while you prepare the batter, stirring occasionally.

Prepare the cake: Preheat the oven to 350°F. Butter a 9-inch round springform pan.

In a small bowl, whisk together the flour, baking powder, and salt. In a large bowl, beat the butter and sugar with an electric mixer on medium speed until fluffy, about 3 minutes. Beat in the egg and vanilla. On low speed, beat in half of the flour mixture, then the milk, and then the last half of the flour mixture.

Transfer the batter to the prepared pan and smooth the top. Dollop the top of the batter with the peanut mixture and spread it out evenly. Bake the cake until the top is caramelized, the cake is set, and a toothpick inserted into the center comes out with moist crumbs attached, 55 to 65 minutes. Cover the cake with foil if it starts to brown too quickly.

Transfer the pan to a wire rack and let cool for 15 minutes, then remove the ring and let the cake cool completely before serving.

PEANUT TOPPING:

6 tablespoons/¾ stick unsalted butter

⅓ cup granulated sugar

3 tablespoons honey

¼ cup heavy cream

6¾ ounces roasted, salted peanuts (1½ cups)

CAKE:

6 tablespoons/¾ stick unsalted butter, at room temperature, plus more for pan

2 cups all-purpose flour

2 teaspoons baking powder

½ teaspoon kosher salt

1 cup granulated sugar

1 large egg, at room temperature

2 teaspoons pure vanilla extract

¾ cup whole milk, at room temperature

Honey Vanilla Spelt Shortcakes

MAKES 8 TO 10

In the Northeast, we wait for months and months, through interminable cold and gray, for full-color produce to come bursting onto the scene. By July, when the farmers' markets are packed with bushels of rosy nectarines, sour cherries that gleam like rubies in the sun, and raspberries not only red but black and golden, too, the pleasure of food shopping is unparalleled. My son's first months of solid food fell right in the fruit dead zone. I couldn't wait to strap him to my chest, head out to Grand Army Plaza, and let him taste everything. I fantasized about letting him gorge on perfectly soft strawberries that fell to juice when he picked them up and bury his face in ripe peaches until he was sticky from head to toe.

There are too many summer delights to limit shortcake to strawberries only. These biscuits will work wonderfully with whatever you've got. The added honey gives them a nutty, earthy sweetness. Serve them warm for breakfast with salty butter or piled with whipped cream and heaps of summer fruit for a grill-side dessert.

After cutting the first round of biscuits, piece the scraps together to form one or two bonus biscuits, but take care not to overwork the dough.

⅓ cup plus 1 tablespoon granulated sugar

Seeds scraped from 1 vanilla bean

2 cups spelt flour

2 cups all-purpose flour, plus more for dusting

1 tablespoon baking powder

½ teaspoon baking soda

¾ teaspoon kosher salt

¾ cup/1½ sticks unsalted butter, frozen and grated on a box grater

1 cup cold buttermilk

½ cup cold heavy cream, plus more for brushing

3 tablespoons honey

Sanding sugar for sprinkling

In a medium bowl, grind the granulated sugar and vanilla bean seeds together with your fingers to evenly disperse them and flavor the sugar. Add the spelt flour, all-purpose flour, baking powder, baking soda, and salt and whisk until well combined.

Add the frozen grated butter and toss to combine. Freeze the mixture if the butter has gotten soft.

In a liquid measuring cup, whisk together the buttermilk, cream, and honey. Add the buttermilk mixture to the cold flour mixture and mix together with a fork. Tip out the dough onto a lightly floured surface and pat into an 8-inch square. Fold the dough over onto itself and then pat it out again to an 8-inch square. On a lightly floured surface, using a 2½-inch round cutter, cut out 7 biscuits and place them at least 2 inches apart on a parchment-lined baking sheet. You can then pat the scraps back together to make 1 or 2 more. Add those to the baking sheet. Cover with plastic wrap and freeze while the oven preheats to 450°F.

Lightly brush only the tops of each biscuit with some cream and sprinkle with sanding sugar. Bake until puffed and golden brown, 12 to 15 minutes. Transfer the biscuits to a wire rack to cool.

TO SERVE:

1½ cups cold heavy cream

1 tablespoon confectioners' sugar

2 pounds fresh fruit, such as raspberries, sugarplums, and gooseberries (4 cups)

1 to 3 tablespoons granulated sugar (depending on the sweetness of the fruit)

When ready to serve, whip the cream and confectioners' sugar to soft peaks. Toss the fruit with the granulated sugar. Split each biscuit, top with some cream and some fruit, and replace the top. Extra biscuits are lovely toasted with butter and jam.

Maple Glazed Doughnuts

MAKES 12 LARGE DOUGHNUTS

My father-in-law walked into the living room where I was working on my laptop and said two words: maple bars. I stopped what I was doing and looked up. I needed more information. He told me that when he was a kid in Dover, New Hampshire, he and his friends would ride their bikes about a mile down the road to the town center. They would always stop by the bakery, where his choice was the maple square. He held up my cell phone as a size reference and called up his memories of the texture of the doughnut—very light—and the glaze—not too thick, not too thin, and just enough.

One of the first independent things we do as children is set out, coins in pocket, to buy treats. I still remember my first solo trip to Denny's with my friend Nikki. We were eight years old. I ordered a stack of pancakes complete with an ice cream–size scoop of butter and plenty of syrup. It's been a few years since then, but the thrill of choosing exactly what you want to eat, paying for it yourself, and indulging without sharing never gets old.

DOUGH:

¾ cup warm whole milk (110°F–115°F)

1 tablespoon active dry yeast

⅓ cup granulated sugar, divided

3½ cups all-purpose flour, plus more for dusting

1 teaspoon kosher salt

2 large eggs, at room temperature

6 tablespoons/¾ stick unsalted butter, at room temperature

1½ quarts (6 cups) vegetable oil for frying

GLAZE:

1 cup pure maple syrup

1 cup confectioners' sugar

1 to 2 tablespoons whole milk

Pinch of kosher salt

Prepare the doughnuts: In a small bowl, combine the milk, yeast, and 1 teaspoon of the granulated sugar. Set aside until foamy, about 5 minutes.

In the bowl of a stand mixer with the dough hook attached, combine the remaining sugar, flour, and salt. With the mixer on low speed, add the yeast mixture and eggs and knead until smooth and elastic, about 5 minutes. Add the butter, a bit at a time, and continue to knead the dough until the butter is fully incorporated and the dough is smooth, another 5 minutes. The dough will be sticky. Scrape down the sides of the bowl and gather the dough into a neat ball. Alternatively, mix together the remaining sugar, flour, and salt in a large bowl, using a wooden spoon. Add the yeast mixture and the eggs and stir to combine. Knead the dough in the bowl until smooth. Knead in the butter pieces until incorporated. Tip out the dough onto a work surface and continue to knead until smooth. Return the dough to the bowl.

Cover with plastic wrap and set aside to rise in a warm place until doubled, 1 to 2 hours. (After the dough has doubled, you can punch it down, wrap it well, and refrigerate for up to 2 days.)

Tip out the dough onto a lightly floured surface and knead it once or twice to expel the air. Cut the dough in half. Working with 1 piece of dough at a time, roll the dough into a 10 x 3½-inch rectangle. Trim the dough to make a neat rectangle, then cut the dough into 6 equal rectangles that are about 1½ x 3½ inches. Transfer the rectangles to a well-floured rimmed baking sheet. Repeat with the remaining dough.

Cover loosely with plastic wrap and set aside to rise in a warm place until almost doubled, about 1 hour.

Line a rimmed baking sheet with 2 layers of paper towels. Clip a candy thermometer to the edge of a 12-inch cast-iron skillet. Heat the oil in the skillet until it reaches 350°F. Carefully transfer 1 piece of dough at a time to a stiff, flat spatula, such as a fish spatula, without deflating it. Then, transfer the dough to the hot oil. Add up to 4 pieces of dough at a time. Maintain the temperature of the oil by increasing or lowering the heat as necessary. Cook the doughnuts for 2½ minutes per side then, using the spatula, transfer the doughnuts to the prepared baking sheet to drain any excess oil. Repeat with the remaining dough.

Prepare the glaze: In a small skillet, bring the maple syrup to a simmer over medium-high heat. Cook until the syrup has reduced by half, about 10 minutes. (Tip it out into a glass measuring cup every so often to check, if you need to.) In a small bowl, whisk together the confectioners' sugar, reduced syrup, 1 tablespoon of the milk, and salt until smooth. Add more milk, if necessary.

Dip the top of each doughnut in the glaze. Serve warm and drippy or let the doughnuts stand at room temperature until the glaze has set.

Raspberry Pineapple Ice Pops
with Lemongrass

MAKES 10 POPS

A pretty woman stood with the toes of her boots on the yellow line marking the edge of the subway platform at the West Fourth Street station. Aboveground, it was pouring, but somehow she looked neat, with a slick ponytail and a classic trench coat, leaning ever so slightly on a large and expensive-looking umbrella. Cuddled close to her right leg was a little girl, maybe four years old, equally tidy in her yellow slicker, both of them waiting patiently. I marveled at how well behaved the child was, what a nice family they must be. Then, the girl's bright eyes darted to the left. Then, to the right. She moved closer to her mother, inching up to the large umbrella. Almost imperceptibly, like a little frog, she licked the cool raindrops off the umbrella and smiled. Then, she did it again, followed by a quick glance around to see who was watching. Mom didn't notice. And neither did anyone else, except me.

I think you'll find the combination of lemongrass and fruit as refreshing as a cool umbrella on a rainy day.

In a small saucepot, bring ½ cup of water and the sugar and lemongrass to a simmer just until the sugar is dissolved, about 1 minute. Cover and set aside to steep for at least 1 hour.

Using a blender or an immersion blender, process the pineapple until smooth. You should have 1 cup of pineapple purée. Blend more pineapple as necessary. Separately, purée the raspberries in the same manner, then strain the through a fine-mesh sieve, pressing on the solids with a spatula, making sure not to waste any purée. You should have 1 cup of seedless raspberry purée.

Strain the lemongrass mixture through a fine-mesh sieve, pressing on the solids to exact as much liquid as possible. Mix half of this syrup with the pineapple purée and half with the raspberry purée. Divide the raspberry purée equally among ten 3-ounce ice pop molds. Then, divide the pineapple mixture equally among the molds. Using a butter knife or a wooden skewer, swirl the 2 purées together just enough to create a pretty swirl. Place the top of each mold on the molds and add the sticks. Freeze until solid, at least 8 to 12 hours.

½ cup granulated sugar

2 lemongrass stalks, trimmed and thinly sliced

¼ small pineapple, peeled and cored

1 pound (about 3 cups) fresh raspberries

Soft Salty Pretzels

MAKES 10 PRETZELS

New Yorkers love to denigrate Times Square. I understand why most people avoid it: It's crowded, it's loud, and it's jam-packed with less-than-desirable smells. I see it differently, though. When my brother, Mohan, was twenty-five, he moved to New York and rented a tiny studio one block from Times Square. He wasn't interested in the trendy Manhattan neighborhoods or the hip Brooklyn spots. He wanted to live near what he considered the epicenter of the city. When I came to visit him, an impressionable and happy twenty-year-old, he told me how exciting life was by his apartment. One evening after dinner, full of a rich meal from his favorite Indonesian restaurant, we walked over to Forty-Second Street. The sun was just going down, and plenty of people were still out and about, but the crowds weren't overwhelming. Together we stood in the middle of Eighth Avenue and did a little spin. The signs sparkled and flashed and changed every second. Tourists were smiling, snapping pictures, eating hot dogs and big, chewy pretzels. My brother was right.

DOUGH:

¾ cup warm water (110° to 115°F)

2¼ teaspoons active dry yeast

3 tablespoons dark brown sugar, divided

3 cups bread flour

2 teaspoons kosher salt

4 tablespoons unsalted butter/ ½ stick, cut into pieces, at room temperature, plus more for bowl

FOR WATER BATH:

⅓ cup baking soda

3 tablespoons dark brown sugar

TO FINISH:

Pretzel salt or flaky sea salt for sprinkling

Prepare the dough: In the bowl of a stand mixer, combine the warm water, yeast, and 1 teaspoon of the brown sugar and let stand until foamy, about 5 minutes.

Add the bread flour, remaining brown sugar, and salt and mix with the paddle attachment until well combined. Switch to the dough hook and mix until a shaggy dough forms, about 3 minutes. Add the butter pieces, a few at a time, and continue to mix the dough until smooth and pliable, 5 to 7 minutes. Alternatively, mix together the ingredients in a large bowl, using a wooden spoon. Knead the dough, in the bowl, until it is shaggy, about 3 minutes. Then, knead in the butter pieces with your hands until incorporated. Tip out the dough onto a work surface and continue to knead until smooth. The dough should be supple and smooth and not too sticky. Remove the dough from the bowl, butter the bowl, and return the dough. Cover with plastic wrap and let stand at room temperature until doubled, 1 to 2 hours. Gently expel the air from the dough, knead it into a ball again, cover with plastic wrap, and refrigerate overnight.

Line two rimmed baking sheets with two silicone baking mats. On a lightly floured surface, cut the dough into 10 equal pieces, about 2½ ounces each. Working with 1 piece a time, roll out to a 16- to 18-inch length. Form into a pretzel shape by first forming the dough into a U, then twisting the ends around each other and bringing them down to overlap over the bottom. Transfer to the prepared baking sheet and repeat with the remaining dough. Set the shaped pretzels aside to puff for about 25 minutes.

Preheat the oven to 425°F.

Prepare the water bath: Bring 8 cups of water to a simmer in a large pot. (Make sure the water is at least a few inches below the rim of the pan as it will bubble furiously when you add the baking soda.) Add the baking soda and the brown sugar to the water and whisk to combine. Once the bubbles have mostly subsided, carefully add 2 or 3 pretzels to the pot. (I think it's easiest to put the pretzel into the bowl of a spider or large slotted spoon and lower it into the water.) Cook for about 30 seconds to 1 minute per side then, using a slotted spoon or spider, transfer them to the prepared baking sheets. Sprinkle with the pretzel salt. Repeat with the remaining pretzels.

Bake the pretzels until puffed and deep golden brown, 15 to 18 minutes. Transfer the baking sheets to a wire rack to cool for a few minutes, if possible.

CHAPTER FOUR

LOVE

Bittersweet

Years ago, back before my ex-husband even became my husband, we were in love, and Lupa was our spot. The night I have in mind was freezing cold, but as we crossed Houston Street on the way to the restaurant I had my right hand tucked into the left pocket of his peacoat, and I felt nothing but warmth. Everything was perfect. Right away, we scored a couple of seats at the bar, no easy feat, especially on a Saturday. Soon other people were packed in around and behind us, waiting impatiently for their tables, so close they could probably smell the pillowy rosemary focaccia on our bread plates.

We ordered wine, but I didn't need it. I'm not much of a drinker to begin with, and I was already dizzy with the pleasure of being with him. We stared like idiots. We smiled like fools. I laughed so hard that I hit my forehead against the edge of my own wineglass. I can only imagine the eye-rolling we inspired.

The pasta at Lupa is my favorite in the city. The portion size is just right, never too big. Each al dente noodle serves a purpose. I especially like to order whatever special pasta the cooks have concocted for the season, most often an unfussy masterpiece with lip-smacking depth. Covered in a slick of buttery sauce, it's never too rich but always plenty decadent. Every bowl is a romp.

I got the special, he got the Bolognese. As we ate, I swayed with the pleasure. I recall pumping my fist with gluttonous delight. A goober in love. And then, I swayed a little too much.

Balance has always been a bit of a problem for me. (Once I flipped over the handlebars of my bike while riding uphill.) In an instant, I saw his smile flatten and his eyebrows rise. I tried to reach out for a handhold, but suddenly I was swimming through pudding. Life always switches to slow motion right when things get embarrassing.

When I started to slip, just a hair, I jammed my foot down to find the bottom rung of my stool. Nothing there. The stool bucked like a horse and I lost control. I threw my hands out, trying to grab anything. Maybe a piece of fluffy focaccia to break the fall. On the way down, I saw his surprise. I saw people turning to stare at me, confused. And then I was down. All the way down. Sitting on the floor, in a crowded restaurant, on a Saturday night in New York City. Shocked and lost for words. Butt bruised. Ego squashed. But laughing.

I stood up and tried to put myself together again. Straightened my stool and remounted. Brushed off the concerned inquiries, shrugged my shoulders, and addressed the business of my special pasta. Happens to everyone, right? I would like to think so.

After we had cleaned our bowls, the bartender slid over small glasses of tawny amaro on the house. The bitter and the sweet, in liquor as in love. It went down easy, the pleasant warmth in my chest dulling the fiery burn I still felt in my cheeks. I was embarrassed, yes, but still in love. And Lord knows, I wasn't half as embarrassed as I would be when I fell down the stairs at the Hustler Club.

But that's a story for another day.

Amaro Stracciatella Ice Cream

MAKES ABOUT 1 QUART ICE CREAM

Amaro is an aged Italian spirit usually enjoyed as a digestif. Made from herbs, citrus, flowers, and spices, it has deep, complex bitter and sweet elements. At first sip, you don't know quite what you've got, but you know you want more. At second sip, the pleasant warmth takes over. By the third, you're in love. *Amaro* means "bitter" in Italian. Love, of course, is *amore*. Not a coincidence, I wouldn't think.

In a medium saucepan, whisk together the milk, cream, and vanilla bean and seeds. Bring the mixture to a boil, then turn off the heat and cover. Let stand for at least 30 minutes.

Set a fine-mesh sieve over a bowl. Whisk the egg yolks, sugar, and salt into the cream mixture. Cook over medium-low heat, stirring constantly, until the mixture is just thick enough to coat the back of a spoon, 6 to 8 minutes. It's important not to let the mixture come to a boil or it will curdle.

Strain the custard through the sieve and discard any solids. Whisk in the amaro. Set the bowl into a larger bowl of ice water. Stir occasionally until completely chilled and very thick. (Alternatively, chill the mixture overnight.) It must be very cold. Set a metal loaf pan into the freezer to chill.

Churn in an ice-cream maker according to the manufacturer's instructions. Halfway through the churning process, melt the chocolate in the microwave in 30-second bursts or in a double boiler. Stir until very smooth, then add the oil and stir to combine. Let it stand until cool to the touch but still pourable. When the ice cream is almost finished, add in the chocolate in a very thin stream. It should solidify and break into shards in the ice cream. Transfer to the chilled loaf pan, cover tightly with plastic wrap, and freeze until firm, at least 6 hours. Let stand for 5 minutes at room temperature before serving.

ICE CREAM:

1 cup milk

3 cups heavy cream

½ vanilla bean, split and seeds scraped

8 large egg yolks

½ cup granulated sugar

½ teaspoon salt

⅓ cup amaro

TO FINISH:

4½ ounces bittersweet chocolate, chopped (1 cup)

4 teaspoons vegetable oil

FORTUNATE

Five thirty p.m. and the sky was already pitch black. The winter wind found its way into the cracks of my scarf, down my collar, and into my bones as I shuffled home down Mulberry Street. Feeling lonely. Feeling low.

There had been a big package delivery and the vestibule was littered with cardboard boxes of varying sizes. Some were already ripped open by hopeful thieves, their tape slashed aggressively and contents laid out for all to see. Most had been toppled and tossed by other residents searching for their own names. Grumpy and tired, I kicked the boxes around with my foot to search, unwilling to remove my hands from my pockets and expose my hands to the draft. My expectations were low.

Then, I saw a small brown box about the size of a brick. For me from Cate.

I adore Cate. It's easy to have a lot of friends you never see. Scheduling is always an issue. Everyone is always busy. I know that Cate is busy, too. But somehow making dates with her was never hard. For years and years, we just fit each other in. When she moved to California, we talked on the phone all the time, but I missed her desperately.

A few days earlier, I had called her in hysterics. I couldn't stop crying. I couldn't get a breath in. Everything was awful. I was four months pregnant and alone. I needed to find an apartment with some room for a crib. I had deadlines looming. But all I could do was lay on my couch and cry. Cate listened and she made me laugh. She stayed on the phone with me until I wasn't desperate any more. She made me promise to make myself a bowl of pasta and go to bed.

I took the box upstairs. I would have ripped it open on way up, but an unsolicited package from a friend is such a rare occurrence. It deserved more attention and care than the special tweezers I had ordered from Amazon the week before. I wanted to sit on my couch and savor it. I shook it and heard a dense, soft rattle but nothing distinguishing. Cate and I have always liked to discuss books we're reading, but the size of this package wasn't right for a book.

Once on the couch, I tore off the packing tape. Inside was a tightly wound ball of green bubble wrap, too many layers to see through. I undid a piece of tape and peeled off a small square of bubble wrap. Funny Cate. One after another I peeled off tiny strips and squares of bubble wrap. It reminded me of a parlor trick. Pieces of bubble wrap multiplied around me but the ball itself refused to shrink. After a lot of serious peeling I came to a miniature version of a white Chinese take-out box adorned with red pagodas. Inside was one perfect homemade fortune cookie. Deep golden brown and expertly folded. I cracked it open to find my fortune handwritten on a tiny slip of pink paper by my dear friend. It said, "You are beloved," and I knew I was.

Dried Fruit and Coconut Florentines

MAKES ABOUT 2 DOZEN COOKIES

A fortune cookie is a wafer cookie made with sugar, flour, egg white, and a little bit of almond extract, which has been folded around a fortune while still warm. We all know how delicious their simple sweetness can be, especially after a rich meal. These florentines remind me of fortune cookies that have been decked out with hazelnuts and almonds to up the crunch factor. They make the perfect treat to wrap up and send to a dear friend exactly when she needs to know that you love her.

1¼ ounces hazelnuts, toasted and skinned (¼ cup)

1¼ ounces raw almonds (¼ cup)

¼ cup granulated sugar

2 tablespoons unsalted butter

1 tablespoon Lyle's Golden Syrup or light corn syrup

2 tablespoons heavy cream

½ teaspoon kosher salt

2 tablespoons all-purpose flour, plus more for dusting

¼ cup shredded unsweetened coconut

1 ounce dried sour cherries, minced (2 tablespoons)

4½ ounces bittersweet chocolate, chopped (1 cup)

In a food processor, combine the hazelnuts, almonds, and sugar and pulse until finely ground.

In a small saucepan, melt the butter over medium heat. Add the golden syrup, cream, salt, and nut mixture. Bring to a boil and cook for 1 minute. Remove from the heat and stir in the flour, coconut, and cherries. Set aside until cool enough to handle but not cold. (If the dough happens to get too cold, it will firm up. Pop it into the microwave for a few 2- to 3-second bursts to soften it.)

Preheat the oven to 350°F. Line 2 rimmed baking sheets with parchment. Scoop the dough into 1-inch balls (about 2 teaspoons). Place the balls, at least 2 inches apart, on the prepared baking sheets. Use a small glass, lightly floured, to press the dough balls into 1¾-inch circles.

Bake until golden around the edges and flat, 8 to 12 minutes. Transfer the baking sheets to a wire rack to cool completely.

Meanwhile, melt the chocolate in a double boiler or in short bursts in a microwave. Spread about a teaspoon of melted chocolate on the flat side of each cookie. Return the cookies, chocolate-side up, to the baking sheets and set aside until the chocolate has set, 30 minutes to 1 hour.

Store the cookies in an airtight container at room temperature for up to 1 week or in the freezer for up to a month.

Brown Sugar and Vanilla Bean Cheesecake

SERVES 8 TO 10

Me, I'll take my cheesecake any which way. Cream cheese–laden, ricotta-lightened, 1990s-style fruit coulis–adorned—I love them all. But this a cheesecake for people who don't like the familiar versions. I first tasted it on a recent trip to Japan: cotton-style cheesecake. My version is more like a soufflé, actually, with a minimal amount of cheese. It's fluffy yet still rich. The simple flavoring makes it a perfect base for ripe strawberries in the summer or orange and grapefruit segments in the winter.

Unsalted butter for pan

6 ounces cream cheese, cut into pieces

½ cup heavy cream

Seeds scraped from ½ vanilla bean

4 large eggs, separated

½ cup cake flour

⅓ cup plus 3 tablespoons packed dark brown sugar, divided

¼ teaspoon cream of tartar

Boiling water

Seasonal fruit for serving

Preheat the oven to 325°F. Bring a kettle of water to a boil. Butter the bottom of an 8-inch-diameter, 2-inch-high round cake pan and line it with parchment.

In a medium bowl set over a small pot of barely simmering water but not touching it, combine the cream cheese, cream, and vanilla bean seeds. Warm the mixture gently, whisking it occasionally until smooth. Remove the bowl from the heat and whisk in the egg yolks, cake flour, and 3 tablespoons of the brown sugar.

In another medium bowl, with an electric mixer on medium speed, beat the egg whites and cream of tartar until opaque with small white bubbles, about 1 minute. While beating, gradually add the remaining ⅓ cup of brown sugar, 1 tablespoon at a time. Continue to beat until you have stiff, shiny peaks, about 4 minutes more.

Mix about a third of the egg white mixture into the cream cheese mixture to loosen it, then gently fold in the remainder. Be careful not to deflate the egg whites. Transfer the batter to the prepared pan and smooth the top. Set the cake pan in a 13 x 9-inch baking pan and add enough boiling water to reach about halfway up the side of the cake pan.

Transfer to the oven and bake until light brown on the top and the center springs back when pressed gently, 60 to 65 minutes. Turn off the oven and leave the cake in the oven with the door closed for another 30 minutes. It will shrink a bit. Remove the baking pan from the oven and let the cake cool completely in its pan in the water.

Carefully flip out the cake onto a flat plate, then flip it right-side up onto a serving plate. Cover it with plastic wrap and refrigerate until completely cold, at least 2 hours. Serve with fruit. Keep leftovers well wrapped and refrigerated for up to 3 days.

Lemon Curd

MAKES ABOUT 1¼ CUPS CURD

A wrinkled Post-it note was smooshed into a corner of my wallet. A vestige of my old life. "See you soon, my loon. I love my gal." It's funny how an artifact from the past can surface from nowhere and unmoor you. How a private language can come to seem so foreign.

Love lost. It happens to everyone, right?

Well, you know what they say. Life gave me a lemon yellow Post-it and I made some curd.

Lemon curd is smelling salt for the soul. Cool and bracingly tart, a thick schmear on toast, a buttery shortbread cookie, or even just a big dollop on a spoon can awaken the senses and maybe even revive a broken heart. Keep a jar handy at all times.

In a medium, heavy-bottomed saucepan, whisk together the egg yolks, egg, and sugar until very well combined. Whisk in the lemon zest and juice. Add the butter and salt.

Heat the mixture over medium heat, stirring constantly with a wooden spoon, until it has thickened, about 5 minutes. You should be able to draw a clear line that holds through the curd on the back of a wooden spoon. (There will be some pieces visible pieces of egg white. Don't worry!) Immediately strain the mixture through a fine-mesh sieve over a small bowl. Discard any solids left behind. Press a piece of plastic or waxed paper into the surface of the curd and chill until ready to use. It will thicken as it cools.

4 large egg yolks

1 large egg

½ cup granulated sugar

2 teaspoons finely grated lemon zest

½ cup freshly squeezed lemon juice (from 3 to 4 lemons)

6 tablespoons/ ¾ stick unsalted butter, cut into pieces

Pinch of kosher salt

Coconut-Scented Vegan Graham Crackers

Our dream vacation to Vieques included touring the island in a jeep, enjoying a private pool at a run-down villa, eating comically bad food, a bedbug scare, and the most heavenly deserted beaches one could ever imagine—all in all, an excellent girls' trip.

One afternoon, we decided to take a horseback ride on the beach. My friends and I trotted along slowly in a line, passing tall coconut palms and mango trees with branches bowed from the weight of ripening fruit. But the highlight of the ride was the end. When we returned to the stable, we learned that most of the horses we rode were new mothers. Their foals were waiting for them in a smaller pen, and once we rounded the final corner and the babies were all in sight again, the mama horses picked up the pace. The foals started neighing frantically and running in circles with delight. And the horses we were riding galloped triumphantly back to their babies with so much speed that we inexperienced riders almost lost our seats. Everyone laughed and cooed. My friend Rosie even cried. I spent the rest of the day trying not to feel guilty about having separated them in the first place.

These graham crackers, made with coconut, are inspired by that tropical ride. Rolling the dough thinly will result in crispier cookies. Roll the dough a little more thickly for softer cookies. But if you do that, you'll have fewer cookies. Baker's choice.

Preheat the oven to 350°F.

In a food processor, process the graham and all-purpose flours, brown sugar, flaxseed meal, baking powder, baking soda, salt, and cinnamon until combined. Add the coconut oil, molasses, and golden syrup and process until combined. Add just 3 tablespoons of the almond milk and pulse until a dough forms. Add more almond milk, as necessary. Divide the dough into 2 portions.

On a piece of parchment, roll 1 rectangle to an even 12½ x 8½ inch-rectangle, about ⅛ inch thick. Trim away about ½ inch from all sides. Cut the rectangle into twelve 4 x 2-inch rectangles, but don't separate the cookies. Score each rectangle in half crosswise but don't cut all the way through. Using a fork, make 3 pricks in each square. Transfer the parchment, with the rolled dough, to a baking sheet. Repeat with the remaining portion of dough.

Bake each scored rectangle until the edges have darkened slightly and the dough is set and dry, about 25 minutes. Remove from the oven. While the rectangles are still warm, use a knife to cut the cookies apart. Transfer the baking sheets to a wire rack to cool completely before removing the individual cookies.

1¼ cups graham flour or whole wheat flour, plus more for dusting

1¼ cups all-purpose flour

½ cup packed light brown sugar

1 tablespoon ground flax-seed meal

1 teaspoon baking powder

½ teaspoon baking soda

½ teaspoon kosher salt

1½ teaspoons ground cinnamon

½ cup melted coconut oil

¼ cup molasses

1 tablespoon Lyle's Golden Syrup or agave syrup

5 to 6 tablespoons almond milk

Hidden Heart Biskvi Cookies

MAKES ABOUT 3 DOZEN COOKIES

In the summer of 1999, I lived in Boston, worked at the Children's Museum, and was too cheap to pay for air-conditioning. On my off days, I would just lay around with an icy spray bottle, dousing myself as necessary to keep from melting. At work, I led tours, put on shows, and made sure no one got stuck in the Big Dig playscape. On some days, especially hot ones, I would have to don a hairy aardvark suit and become Arthur, the beloved PBS cartoon character, to greet children on the street.

I would have hated it, except for the children. They squealed with joy when I waved and ran into my arms, grinning wildly at the unfailing magic of it. Sometimes, they would plant their chubby hands on either side of the cartoon head and whisper secrets and loving messages into the giant mesh eyeholes. Under those sweaty layers of felt and plaster, my real heart swelled.

A Swedish biskvi cookie is a multilayered delight made up of an almond macaroon base, a dense scoop of chocolate buttercream, and a thin chocolate shell. My raspberry version was inspired by those heartwarming days in Boston. These cookies aren't hard to make, but they require a few more steps than the average chocolate chipper. If you like, make the cookies and the buttercream a day in advance to break up the process.

COOKIES:

3 cups sliced almonds (12 ounces)

1 cup granulated sugar

2 large egg whites

1 teaspoon almond extract

½ teaspoon kosher salt

BUTTERCREAM:

⅔ cup granulated sugar

3 large egg whites

1 cup/2 sticks unsalted butter, at room temperature, cut into pieces

⅓ cup raspberry jam

TO FINISH:

¼ cup raspberry jam

6 ounces fresh raspberries (1 cup)

Prepare the cookies: Preheat the oven to 350°F. Line 2 rimmed baking sheets with parchment paper.

In a food processor, combine the almonds and sugar and process until the nuts are finely ground. Add the egg whites, almond extract, and salt and process until you have a sticky dough that starts to clump together into a ball around the blade.

Drop the dough by 1-tablespoon scoops, spacing them about ½ inch apart, onto the prepared pans. With slightly damp hands, roll the scoops into neat balls, then press down into even 1½-inch circles. Bake the cookies until they look dry and set and the edges are just beginning to brown, about 18 minutes, rotating the sheets halfway through baking. Transfer the baking sheets to wire racks to cool the cookies completely. Use an offset spatula, if necessary, to lift each cooled cookie off of the parchment.

Prepare the buttercream: Whisk together the sugar and egg whites in the bowl of a stand mixer or a large bowl. Set the bowl over a pot of barely simmering water, making sure the bottom of the bowl doesn't touch the water. Whisk the mixture over the heat until the sugar is completely

(continued on page 134)

12 ounces bittersweet chocolate, not chips, chopped (about 3 cups)

2 teaspoons vegetable oil

dissolved and the mixture is warm, about 3 minutes. Rub some of the mixture between your fingers to make sure the sugar has dissolved completely. Transfer the bowl to the stand mixer fitted with the whisk attachment or use an electric mixer on medium-high speed to beat until you have stiff, glossy peaks and the mixture has cooled to almost room temperature, about 5 minutes.

Reduce the speed to medium-low and add the butter, a piece or two at a time, and beat until smooth. If you're using a stand mixer, switch to the paddle attachment about halfway through adding the butter. Beat until smooth and creamy and lovely, then beat in the jam. Don't worry if the mixture is loose; it will firm up as you continue to beat it. (If it curdles, and doesn't smooth out over time, apply a little gentle heat to the underside of the bowl. A mini blowtorch works well. Or use a dish towel soaked with hot water.)

To finish the cookies, set the 2 racks of cookies over rimmed baking sheets. Spread a bit of raspberry jam on each cookie, then top with a raspberry. Use a small cookie scoop or a piping bag to top each cookie with about 2 tablespoons of buttercream. Pop these into the fridge to set up before moving on, about 10 minutes.

Melt the chocolate with the oil in a double boiler or in short bursts in the microwave, stirring often. Carefully spoon the chocolate mixture over each cookie to cover the buttercream completely. Chill until the chocolate is firm, about 25 minutes. Serve at cold or at room temperature, but store leftovers in an airtight container in the fridge.

Caramel Cookie Bars

MAKES 48 COOKIES

Doris and Lamont lived across the street from my family on our suburban cul-de-sac. Their children were grown and they lived alone. I would use their driveway for biking (it had a superior hill) and their lawn for exploring. When I got tired and needed some grandmotherly affection, I would open the screen door and let myself in to their pale blue living room. Doris always obliged. We sipped on big, frosty glasses of lemonade and played countless games of checkers while we chatted. Her delicious southern accent sounded like pure love. I marveled at the fact she could decorate her home with crystal dishes full of colorful candy and not spend all day eating it. Little candy bars and sparkling Starlight Mints called to me from all corners. Decorating with candy? How mature.

These homey cookies remind me of the ones that adorned Doris's house. You should serve them in your most grandmotherly crystal dishes, if you can. Mine never seem to make it that far.

COOKIE BASE:

½ cup/1 stick unsalted butter, at room temperature (but not too soft), plus more for pan

1¼ cups all-purpose flour

¼ cup confectioners' sugar

¼ cup dark packed brown sugar

½ teaspoon kosher salt

CARAMEL:

1 cup granulated sugar

½ cup heavy cream

2 tablespoons unsalted butter

¾ teaspoon kosher salt

TO FINISH:

12 ounces bittersweet chocolate, chopped (about 3 cups)

Prepare the cookie base: Preheat the oven to 350°F. Butter a 9-inch square baking pan and line with parchment paper, leaving a 2-inch overhang on 2 opposite sides.

In a large bowl, beat the flour, confectioners' sugar, brown sugar, and salt on medium speed until well combined. Add the butter and beat until the crumbs are evenly moistened but still sandy. Tip the crumbs into the prepared pan and using the flat underside of a ¼-cup measuring cup press down into an even layer. Bake the base until lightly golden and set, about 20 minutes. Transfer the pan to a wire rack to cool.

Prepare the caramel: Place the granulated sugar in a medium saucepan. Cook over medium-high heat, without stirring (although you can gently swirl the pan, if necessary), until the caramel is medium amber in color, 5 to 6 minutes. Clip a candy thermometer to the side of the pan and then slowly add the cream; be very careful, it will bubble up and spatter. Stir in the butter and salt. Cook until the mixture reaches 248°F. Immediately pour the caramel over the cookie base. Lift and tilt the pan to spread the caramel evenly over the base. Let stand until cool and set, about 1 hour.

Using the parchment overhang as handles, lift the cookie slab out of the pan and onto a cutting board. Using a serrated knife, cut into 48 pieces. Line 2 baking sheets with parchment paper.

If you'd like to cover these cookies in tempered chocolate, flip to page 7 for instructions. Otherwise, melt the chocolate in a double boiler or in short bursts in a microwave. Working with few cookies at a time, dip them into the melted chocolate and toss them around with a fork to coat. Use the fork to lift out each piece and tap it against the side of the bowl to remove any excess chocolate. Transfer the coated cookies to the prepared baking sheets. Pop the sheets into the fridge to harden, about 30 minutes. Serve cold or at room temperature.

Hummocky Meadow Berry Buckle

SERVES 8

The rolling hills glowed green. Add in the bluest sky, slate-sharp snow-capped peaks, and sleepy slow cows ding-a-linging as they ambled, and I had to pinch myself to keep from singing "The Sound of Music." We were on a romantic trip to the German Alps, and I was drinking it all in like smooth, creamy milk. The grassy slopes were pocked with little humps, making the whole scene even more adorably Hobbity. From a well-placed bilingual sign, I learned that we were in a hummocky meadow, which is as nice a place to be as it sounds. The hummocks form when the earth below shifts. Or something like that. I'm not a geologist. All I could think about was how that hummocky meadow reminded me of a pistachio-covered cake, made irregular by fruit sinking in and bubbling below the surface.

If you're using frozen wild blueberries, don't thaw them before adding them to the batter. Just note that the cake will take a little longer to bake.

STREUSEL:

¼ cup all-purpose flour

¼ cup old-fashioned rolled oats

¼ teaspoon baking powder

2 tablespoons light brown sugar

¼ teaspoon kosher salt

3 tablespoons unsalted butter, at room temperature but not too soft

2½ ounces raw pistachios, very finely chopped (½ cup)

CAKE:

6 tablespoons/ ¾ stick unsalted butter, at room temperature, plus more for pan

1½ cups all-purpose flour

1 teaspoon baking powder

¾ teaspoon kosher salt

¼ teaspoon baking soda

¾ cup granulated sugar

2 large eggs, at room temperature

Preheat the oven to 350°F.

Prepare the streusel: In a medium bowl, combine the flour, oats, baking powder, brown sugar, and salt. Add the butter and knead it into the flour mixture with your fingers until it is evenly moistened. Add the pistachios and toss to combine. Set aside.

Prepare the cake: Butter a 10-inch oven-safe skillet or cast-iron pan. In a small bowl, whisk together the flour, baking powder, salt, and baking soda. In a large bowl, beat the butter and granulated sugar with an electric mixer on medium speed until light and fluffy, about 2 minutes. Add the eggs, 1 at a time, and the vanilla. Alternate adding the flour mixture and the sour cream, beginning and ending with the flour mixture. Fold in half of the berries. Transfer the batter to the prepared pan and smooth the top. Sprinkle with the remaining berries, then top with the streusel mixture, squeezing it into small clumps. Bake until a toothpick inserted into the center comes out with moist crumbs attached, 45 to 55 minutes. Serve warm.

1 teaspoon pure
vanilla extract

½ cup sour cream, at
room temperature

2 pounds wild blueberries,
fresh or frozen but not
thawed (about 6 cups)

We Are Nuts About Nuts Cookies

MAKES ABOUT 2½ DOZEN SANDWICH COOKIES

These cookies are named after one of my favorite stores: We Are Nuts About Nuts. That was the name on the placard out front. Not "Nuts about Nuts" or "We're Nuts for Nuts." No contractions. No shortcuts. It was a full, proper sentence and I loved it. Unhappily, We Are Nuts About Nuts recently closed after 40 years. But that's a good run.

This cookie is adaptable. Use whichever nut you are nuts about.

Prepare the cookies: In a large bowl, combine the butter and confectioners' sugar; beat with an electric mixer on high speed until fluffy, 2 to 3 minutes. Add the egg yolks and mix to combine. Add the flour and salt, and mix on low speed until incorporated. Divide the dough in half, wrap each portion in plastic wrap, and press into a flat rectangle. Refrigerate until firm, at least 1 hour or overnight.

Preheat the oven to 350°F. Line 2 baking sheets with parchment paper and set aside. Dust a piece of parchment with flour, and roll out 1 portion of dough to a ⅛-inch thickness. Using a 2 x 1-inch rectangle cookie cutter, cut out about 30 cookies. Alternatively, cut the dough into rectangles, using a sharp paring knife. Repeat with the other portion of dough. (You can reroll the scraps once.) Place the rectangles on another baking sheet and freeze until firm, about 10 minutes.

Transfer the frozen rectangles to the prepared baking sheets, placing them about 1 inch apart. Bake, rotating the sheets once halfway through baking, until light golden brown around the edges, 10 to 12 minutes. Transfer the cookies to a wire rack to cool completely.

Prepare the filling: Place the nuts, granulated sugar, and salt in a food processor and pulse until very finely ground. Add the butter and pulse until smooth. Add the Kirsch (if using) and pulse until blended. Transfer to a pastry bag fitted with a ½-inch tip.

Set a wire rack into a rimmed baking sheet. Melt the chocolate. Dip the bottom of half of the cookies in chocolate and set on the rack. Sprinkle some of the chopped nuts over the chocolate. Chill until the chocolate is firm, about 30 minutes.

Turn the remaining cookies bottom up and pipe or spread about 1½ teaspoons of filling onto each cookie. Top with the chocolate half. If not serving immediately, store the cookies, well wrapped, in the fridge.

COOKIES:

¾ cup/1½ sticks unsalted butter, at room temperature

1¼ cups confectioners' sugar

3 large egg yolks

2 cups all-purpose flour, plus more for dusting

¾ teaspoon kosher salt

FILLING:

4 ounces raw nuts, such as pistachios, pecans, or hazelnuts (1 cup)

½ cup granulated sugar

½ teaspoon kosher salt

4 tablespoons/½ stick unsalted butter, at room temperature

1 to 2 teaspoons Kirsch (optional)

TO FINISH:

4½ ounces milk or dark chocolate, chopped (1 cup)

1 ounce raw nuts, chopped (whichever you used in the filling) (¼ cup)

Orange Streusel Cake

SERVES 16

Walking down Seventh Avenue in Park Slope recently, I spotted a lantana plant at the Bad Wife bodega. Its tall and skinny green stalks end in tiny clusters of flowers that resemble tiny bursts of fireworks, all shades of orange and yellow and red. Gaudy to some but lovely to me and my grandmother, who had lantana lining the dusty walkways through her confetti-colored garden in Sri Lanka. Alongside the lush plumeria, with its canary and cream blossoms, and the cherry red stalks of ginger, they matched the vibrant saris she wore and the floral dishware and bright drapery she chose. I am just like her.

This cake is for her. Shades of orange were her favorite, so I decided to throw the entire orange into the cake, rind and all. A little bold maybe, and if so, good.

STREUSEL:

½ cup all-purpose flour

½ cup packed light brown sugar

¼ teaspoon kosher salt

4 tablespoons/ ½ stick unsalted butter, melted

2 ounces sliced almonds (½ cup)

CAKE:

6 tablespoons/¾ stick unsalted butter, at room temperature, plus more for pan

1 entire organic navel orange (about 10 ounces), scrubbed and cut into large chunks and seeded (yes, rind and all!)

¼ cup sour cream, at room temperature

1½ cups all-purpose flour

1 teaspoon baking powder

½ teaspoon kosher salt

¼ teaspoon baking soda

¾ cup granulated sugar

2 large eggs, at room temperature

Preheat the oven to 350°F.

Prepare the streusel: In a medium bowl, combine the flour, brown sugar, and salt. Drizzle the melted butter over the mixture and stir to incorporate. The mixture should clump together when squeezed. Toss in the almonds.

Prepare the cake: Butter an 8-inch square baking pan. Line the pan with parchment paper, leaving a 2-inch overhang on 2 opposite sides. Butter the parchment.

Place the orange in a blender and process until it is the texture of applesauce. It's okay if you have a few larger pieces. You should have about 1 cup of orange purée. (If you have more than that, add a little seltzer or Champagne to the excess and treat yourself.) Add the sour cream and stir to combine.

In a medium bowl, whisk together the flour, baking powder, salt, and baking soda. In a large bowl, with an electric mixer on medium speed, beat the butter and granulated sugar until light and fluffy, about 3 minutes. Add the eggs, 1 at a time, scraping down the bowl as necessary. Add half of the flour mixture and beat on low speed until just combined. Beat in the orange mixture, then beat in the remaining half of the flour mixture.

Transfer the batter to the prepared pan and smooth the top. Top with the streusel mixture. Squeeze the streusel to form a range of differently sized clumps. Bake until a toothpick inserted into the center of the cake comes out with moist crumbs attached, 40 to 45 minutes. Transfer the pan to a wire rack to cool for 20 minutes. Then, using the parchment overhang as handles, transfer the cake to a wire rack to cool completely.

Prepare the glaze (if using): In a small bowl, whisk the orange juice into

GLAZE (OPTIONAL):
3 to 4 teaspoons freshly
squeezed orange juice
(from 1 orange)
¾ cup confectioners' sugar

the confectioners' sugar, adding a little less juice for a thicker glaze that will look lovely on top of the cake, or a little more for a thinner glaze that will soak in. Drizzle the glaze over the cooled cake.

Store leftovers in an airtight container for up to 3 days, or freeze them for up to 1 week. Thaw before serving.

Raspberry Rhubarb Streusel Muffins

MAKES 12 MUFFINS

My childhood kitchen had barstool seating. It was as if my parents knew that my brother and I would be interested in watching them as they cooked. Truth be told, we just wanted to be near them whenever we could. Sometimes when my mother was chopping vegetables or stirring a pot, I would lean over the counter and stare at her without blinking. Creepy? Yes. When she asked me what the heck I was doing, I always had the same response. "I'm admiring your face." And I was. I thought she was so beautiful that I wanted to soak her in through my eyeballs. She'd laugh and shoo me away.

He doesn't need to admire my face, but I hope my son likes to be near me in the kitchen. I like to think about what we might bake together when he's ready. Muffins would be perfect. I imagine his sweet hands squeezing streusel or stirring batter. I'm sure he would steal a few raspberries, his favorite.

Preheat the oven to 400°F. Line a standard 12-well muffin tin with paper liners.

Prepare the streusel: In a medium bowl, whisk together the flour, brown sugar, and salt until combined. Knead in the butter until the flour mixture is evenly moistened. Set aside.

Prepare the batter: In a small bowl, gently toss 2 tablespoons of the flour with the raspberries. In another medium bowl, whisk together the remaining flour, baking powder, baking soda, and salt. In a large bowl, with an electric mixer on medium speed, beat the butter, granulated sugar, and lime zest until light and fluffy, about 4 minutes. Add the eggs, 1 at a time, beating in between each addition and scraping down the bowl as necessary. Beat in half of the flour mixture just until combined, beat in the buttermilk, then beat in the remaining flour mixture. Do not overbeat. Fold in the rhubarb until even distributed. Then, carefully fold in the floured raspberries, taking as much care as possible not to smash them.

Divide the batter evenly among the prepared cups. Sprinkle the top of each muffin with granulated sugar, then divide the streusel evenly among the muffin tops. Make sure to use up all the streusel.

Bake until the muffins have puffed and a toothpick inserted into the center of a muffin comes out with moist crumbs attached, 18 to 20 minutes. Transfer the pan to a wire rack to cool for 5 minutes, then transfer the muffins to the rack to cool completely.

STREUSEL:

½ cup all-purpose flour

¼ cup packed dark or light brown sugar

¼ teaspoon kosher salt

4 tablespoons/ ½ stick unsalted butter, at room temperature

BATTER:

2 cups all-purpose flour, divided

6 ounces fresh raspberries, halved if large (1 cup)

2¼ teaspoons baking powder

½ teaspoon baking soda

½ teaspoon kosher salt

½ cup/1 stick unsalted butter, at room temperature

¾ cup granulated sugar, plus more for sprinkling

1 teaspoon finely grated lime zest (from 1 lime)

2 large eggs, at room temperature

¾ cup buttermilk, at room temperature

5 ounces rhubarb, diced small (1 cup)

Tavern-Style Blueberry Pancakes

MAKES 12 SMALL PANCAKES

We sat at a table by the window at the Red Lion Inn in Stockbridge. It had a white linen tablecloth and fancy china. It looked like the perfect setting for a proper afternoon tea, but we were eating breakfast. A meaningful breakfast. I ordered a vegetable omelet and he got the malted blueberry pancakes. My omelet was a little too buttery, but his pancakes were just right. In between deep stares and our team effort on the crossword puzzle, I reached over to steal bites. I wondered whether this was all really happening. Were we really going to live happily ever after? Was it possible to be this happy? Could these pancakes really be so delicious?

It turns out that the answer to all but one of those questions is no. I will always remember those pancakes with great fondness.

For extra malty goodness, whisk 2 tablespoons of malted milk powder into ½ cup of hot maple syrup to serve.

2 cups all-purpose flour

½ cup malted milk powder

2 tablespoons granulated sugar

1 teaspoon baking powder

½ teaspoon baking soda

½ teaspoon kosher salt

1½ cups buttermilk, at room temperature

4 tablespoons/½ stick unsalted butter, melted and cooled slightly, plus more for pan

2 large eggs

1½ cups fresh wild blueberries (9 ounces)

Preheat the oven to 200°F.

In a medium bowl, whisk together flour, malted milk powder, sugar, baking powder, baking soda, and salt. In a second medium bowl, whisk together buttermilk, butter, and eggs. Add the buttermilk mixture to the flour mixture and whisk again just until combined. The batter should be slightly lumpy. Fold in half of the blueberries.

Melt a pat of butter in a large, nonstick skillet over medium-high heat. Working in batches, drop about ¼ cup of batter into the skillet to form each pancake. Sprinkle the tops with a few more berries. Cook until small bubbles appear, 3 to 4 minutes. Flip the pancakes and cook until risen and golden brown, adjusting the heat as needed, 2 to 5 minutes more. Transfer to a baking sheet to keep warm in the oven. Repeat with more butter, the remaining batter, and the remaining blueberries, wiping the skillet clean with a paper towel between batches.

CHAPTER FIVE

Wisdom

JFK

John F. Kennedy International Airport is never where I want to be. But recently I figured out something essential about going to the airport. Departures is the wrong end of the equation. The good stuff is at Arrivals. It's just the place for anyone who needs a boost.

Arrivals doesn't look great at first glance. There isn't much to eat. No bookshops to browse. No expensive scarves and bags to covet. But shopping and dining isn't the point. Arrivals is all about the crowd along the barriers.

The crowd is a wave. It grows slowly, gaining force invisibly, until a flight lands and it comes up on the board. Then, the energy crests. Loved ones and livery drivers surge against the barrier. The feeling of hopefulness is palpable. There are flowers. Tears. People find their people and head out. The wave recedes. Over and over again, a beautiful, hypnotic pattern.

A flight from Seoul emerges and I watch as a tiny pigtailed peanut makes her way out first. She is running with her arms outstretched, yelling "Daddy." He runs to the barrier and lifts her up and over it into a hug. I actually cry.

Then, I see a lovely pregnant woman and her husband greet her parents, who obviously haven't yet seen her in that condition. Another tearjerker! Then a little comedy: a pair of older travelers stop in their tracks, blocking the whole line of traffic, looking utterly confused, squinting into the crowd, tripping people around them with their unsteady rolling suitcases.

Next comes a flight from somewhere beachy—somewhere everyone would have liked to stay. The tan faces look hilariously bummed to be returning, which perhaps explains all the duty-free liquor that crowd is hauling.

Finally, I see *my* person. She looks tired. Her hair is just a little more unruly than she usually keeps it. Her eyes are heavy. But she has come to me and I am bursting. To tell her so, I have made her a chocolate and banana cream pie with a salty oat crust—a great big hug in pastry form.

A far cry from the banana cream pies that rotate in backlit cases in diners across the country, this one was made with one person in mind. The crust recalls those perfect British digestive biscuits, a little bit salty, a little bit sweet, and full of crunch. The silky custard is a counterpoint: cool and refreshing, rich with floral essence of a good vanilla bean. It nestles up tight to the dark chocolate and fresh whipped cream. And finally bananas, sliced lengthwise and bedded down in the whole beautiful, creamy mess.

My weary traveler is ready for a shower and a snack. That's fine with me. No talking necessary. The pie says everything I want to say. Welcome home. I'm so happy you're here. I love you. Eat.

Banana B-Oat Cream Pie

SERVES 8 TO 10

While I know that carrot sticks and hummus could be a worthwhile snack after a long journey, I have learned that a slice of pie and a cup of tea are far more soothing. To be virtuous after a journey is overrated. Custard and bananas are not.

As she ate, I asked my friend what I should call this pie. She said, "I'm just glad I can call it mine."

CRUST:

⅔ cup all-purpose flour, plus more for dusting

½ cup old-fashioned rolled oats

1 tablespoon granulated sugar

¾ teaspoon kosher salt

½ cup/1 stick cold unsalted butter, cut into ½-inch pieces

¼ cup ice water

FILLINGS:

3½ cups whole milk

Seeds scraped from 1 vanilla bean

4½ ounces semisweet chocolate, chopped (1 cup)

2 tablespoons heavy cream

5 large egg yolks

⅓ cup granulated sugar

¼ cup cornstarch

½ teaspoon kosher salt

2 tablespoons unsalted butter, cut into pieces

TO FINISH:

3 small bananas, sliced thinly on a deep bias, divided

1½ cups heavy cream

3 to 4 tablespoons confectioners' sugar

Prepare the crust: In a food processor, combine the flour, oats, granulated sugar, and salt. Process until the oats are finely ground. Add the butter and pulse until the mixture resembles coarse meal with some larger pieces. Add the ice water and pulse until the dough is evenly moistened. At this point, stop the processor and feel the dough. If it doesn't hold together when you squeeze it in your hand, you can add a little bit more water. But be careful not to make the dough too wet; it should be a touch crumbly but hold together when squeezed. Tip the mixture onto a piece of plastic wrap. Use the sides of the plastic wrap to gently gather the dough into a ball. Wrap and flatten the dough into a disk. Refrigerate at least 2 hour or up to 3 days.

Preheat the oven to 375°F. On a lightly floured surface, roll out the pastry to a 12-inch-diameter circle. Ease the dough into a standard 9-inch pie plate, trim off any excess, and fold and crimp the edges. Cover with plastic wrap and freeze until firm, about 15 minutes.

Transfer the frozen pie shell to a baking sheet. Line the pie with foil or parchment and fill with pie weights or beans. Bake until the edges are set, about 30 minutes. Remove the pie weights and parchment and bake the empty crust until the edges are golden and the bottom looks dry and set, another 20 to 25 minutes. Transfer the pan to a wire rack to cool completely.

Meanwhile, prepare the fillings: Bring the milk and vanilla bean and seeds to a boil in a large saucepan over medium-high heat, stirring occasionally. Remove from the heat and cover. Let the mixture stand for 30 minutes.

Meanwhile, in short bursts in a microwave or in a double boiler over medium heat, melt the chocolate with the cream and stir until smooth. Pour into the cooled crust and spread evenly over the bottom and sides.

Set a fine mesh sieve over a medium bowl. In a medium bowl, whisk together the egg yolks, granulated sugar, cornstarch, and salt. Add the infused milk a little at a time, to create a smooth mixture. Return the mixture to the pot and heat, stirring, over medium-low heat until thickened, about 10 minutes. Pour through the sieve and discard any solids left behind. Add the butter and let the custard stand for 2 minutes, then whisk until smooth. Pour half of the custard over the chocolate in the crust. Top with 1 sliced banana, then cover completely with the remaining custard. (You don't want any air hitting the banana.) Cover with plastic wrap and refrigerate for at least 6 hours or up to overnight.

Just before serving, top the pie with the remaining 2 bananas, arranging the slices in an overlapping pattern. Beat the cream with the confectioners' sugar to soft peaks. Top the chilled pie with the whipped cream.

LET'S SCREAM FOR ICE CREAM

Completely by accident, I bought the large-print version of *The Book of Joy*, a guide to finding lasting happiness. Somehow the large print makes reading it even more joyful. The trees outside the open window have finally popped green, the breeze is delicious, and I'm sitting on the couch letting the big, soft words wash over me. My eyes are practically slurping up the pages.

Yet as much as I admire the premise of the book, I can't agree with everything. I mean, I definitely see the wisdom in learning to accept pain. Been there. And I chuckle with recognition when I read the very succinct and by-now-obvious-to-me point that dejection in the face of hardship is a waste of time. If something can be done, do it and stop being unhappy. I'm with you guys so far, making sense of the difficult stuff.

What gives me pause is the way the authors talk about pleasure. According to these wisest men, temporary enjoyment can come through the senses, but it's only fleeting, not the source of permanent satisfaction. But I have to wonder: Can't those little moments build into something larger? Suffering is inevitable, certainly, but life is equally filled with moments of pleasure, if you know how to see them and let them in. So I, for one, choose to remain open to the possibility of cumulative sensory joy. Sometimes it's all you've got.

Consider food, as I love to do. The authors suggest that we should eat for nourishment, without attachment and without greed. That sounds very noble and high-minded, but why must we deny the animal and earthly pleasure of food and eating? Dear authors, have you ever ridden your bike, orange robes flapping in the wind, to get an ice-cream cone at the local dairy farm on a warm summer evening? Have you stood outside as the sun goes down, letting the ice cream melt and soften, sweetness and cream cooling your lips and tongue, while the aroma of warm, freshly cut grass fills your nostrils and your heart? The point is not that I love ice cream (though I do), and I'm no more a hedonist than is anyone else who makes desserts for a living. It's not even the ice cream itself that matters, but the way it shows you how damn lucky you are to be alive.

If desire is the root of suffering, as Buddha says, then maybe digging deeper into smaller, attainable pleasures makes some sense as a way of life. I think of pleasurable moments as bricks. One brick is being able to make enough congee for both me and my exhausted and hungry girlfriend who just had a baby. Another brick is when a beloved friend comes over for tea and cookies and wraps her arms around me tightly and unexpectedly. Another brick is the greasy hot hand-pulled noodles I devoured alone at Xian Famous Foods. With each brick, I work at building a world I love to live in.

Strawberries and Cream Ice Cream

MAKES ABOUT 1 QUART ICE CREAM

We played kickball in the street. Just like you see in the movies of America in the olden days. The kids, ranging from ages 5 to 15, and hailing from countries from Egypt to Jamaica, played rowdy games right in the middle of the road. We lived on a dead end, so traffic wasn't an issue. Older brothers helped little sisters. Cousins joined in when they were visiting. Games lasted from just after breakfast until the sun started to set just before dinner. The only thing that could disband the crowd was the ice-cream truck. Like a piece of glass shattering into a million pieces, the beloved sound of the truck jingling up the street would send all the kids immediately scattering to their individual houses to procure change. I remember the anxiety of hoping I could grab 75 cents fast enough and then bolt back to the road in time to buy an a strawberry shortcake ice-cream bar. The five minutes that passed after the truck came through were the quietest and dreamiest minutes the cul-de-sac ever saw. If that's not one of the purest joys known to man, then I don't know what is.

The better the strawberries, the better the ice cream, so it's important to source sweet, fragrant fruit. Eat this ice cream in big scoops or use it as the center of the Neapolitan Ice-Cream Cake (page 90).

Set the strawberries and ¼ cup of the sugar in a fine-mesh sieve over a medium bowl and toss to combine. Set aside to drain for at least 4 hours. Save the remaining strawberry syrup to serve over pancakes or mix into sparkling water and cocktails. Process the macerated berries in a blender until smooth.

In a small saucepan, heat the milk and remaining ¾ cup of sugar over medium-low heat until warm. Add the cream cheese and powdered milk and stir until smooth. Remove from the heat and stir in the cream, salt, and strawberry purée. Transfer to a bowl, cover, and chill until completely cold, at least 8 hours. Set a metal loaf pan in the freezer to chill.

Process the mixture in an ice-cream maker according to the manufacturer's instructions. Transfer to the chilled loaf pan, cover tightly with plastic wrap, and freeze until firm, at least 6 hours. Let stand for 5 minutes at room temperature before serving.

1 pound ripe strawberries, hulled and chopped (about 3 cups)

1 cup granulated sugar, divided

1 cup whole milk

4 ounces cream cheese, at room temperature, cut into pieces

½ cup powdered milk

2 cups heavy cream

½ teaspoon kosher salt

Apple Snack Cake

SERVES 8

It happens so fast here—the shift from summer to fall. All of a sudden, the color of the morning light is different and a scarf becomes more of a necessity than an accessory. This shift also brings loads of apples to the supermarket. Lined up in neat bags, they look as if they've just been picked, whether they have or not. I think it's a scam. Those first bags of Macintosh apples look good but never taste good. Sometimes I think grocery store owners are just capitalizing on the fall fever and selling us old apples from last year. The bags clutter the shelves of my fridge as I add to them every week in a fruitless (ha!) search for crispness.

This cake is my best defense against less-than-perfect apples. Save the crunchy beauties, when they finally come, for eating out of hand.

Unsalted butter for pan

½ cup whole wheat flour

½ cup all-purpose flour

2 teaspoons baking powder

1 teaspoon ground cinnamon

¾ teaspoon kosher salt

¼ teaspoon baking soda

2 large eggs

½ cup packed dark brown sugar

¼ cup granulated sugar

½ cup sour cream

⅓ cup vegetable oil

1½ teaspoons pure vanilla extract

¾ cup unsweetened, shredded coconut

2 ounces chopped pecans (½ cup)

2½ ounces dried currants (½ cup)

2 cups peeled, cored, and diced apples (from about 3 small apples)

Confectioners' sugar for dusting

Preheat the oven to 350°F. Butter a 9-inch-diameter, 2-inch-deep round cake pan and line the bottom with parchment. Butter the parchment.

In a medium bowl, whisk together the whole wheat flour, all-purpose flour, baking powder, cinnamon, salt, and baking soda.

In a large bowl, whisk together the eggs, brown sugar, granulated sugar, sour cream, vegetable oil, and vanilla. Fold in the coconut, pecans, and currants, making sure the currants have separated and the mixture is well combined. Next, fold in the apples, and then the flour mixture.

Transfer the batter to the prepared pan. Bake until the cake is deep golden brown and a toothpick inserted into the center comes out with moist crumbs attached, 40 to 50 minutes. Transfer the pan to a wire rack to cool for 20 minutes.

Cut around the edges of the cake to loosen it. Flip the cake out onto a plate and then carefully flip it back, right-side up, onto a wire rack to cool completely. Dust with confectioners' sugar to serve.

Barley Oat Biscuits

MAKES 2 DOZEN BISCUITS

My friend B has a wonderful habit. If we are sitting around a plate of cheese and crackers, which we often are, B is likely to slice a piece of cheese, place it on a cracker, and hand it to you. The treat always arrives before you've realized that you wanted a piece of cheese on a cracker, and it makes you feel so special. B isn't a mind reader. She's just a sweet and lovely friend, and she knows something true: Most people would always like a snack, especially if someone else makes it for them.

While tasty on their own, these lightly sweetened, crunchy biscuits make a perfect vehicle for a piece of cheese or a schmear of peanut butter.

¼ cup plus 2 tablespoons packed dark brown sugar

2 ounces pecan halves (½ cup)

1 cup quick-cooking oats

½ cup barley flour

½ cup all-purpose flour, plus more for dusting

1¼ teaspoons kosher salt

10 tablespoons/1¼ sticks cold unsalted butter, cut into pieces

2 to 4 tablespoons ice water

2 to 3 tablespoons heavy cream, as needed for brushing

3 to 4 tablespoons granulated sugar, as needed, for sprinkling

In a food processor, combine the brown sugar and pecan halves and process until the nuts are finely ground. Add the oats, barley flour, all-purpose flour, and salt and pulse to incorporate.

Add the butter and pulse until the mixture is the texture of coarse meal, with some slightly larger pieces of butter. Add 2 tablespoons of the ice water and pulse just until the dough is evenly moistened. It should hold together when you squeeze it in your hands, but not be too wet. Add up to 2 more tablespoons of water as necessary.

Divide the dough in half, wrap each portion in plastic wrap, and shape each into a rectangle. Chill the dough for at least 1 hour.

Preheat the oven to 375°F. Line 2 rimmed baking sheets with parchment paper. On a lightly floured surface, working with 1 piece of dough, roll out into a 12 x 6-inch rectangle. Cut the dough into 12 equal rectangles. Transfer the rectangles to 1 of the prepared baking sheets. Brush with cream and sprinkle with granulated sugar. Bake until golden brown around the edges, 18 to 20 minutes. Meanwhile, repeat with the remaining dough.

Transfer the biscuits to a wire rack to cool completely.

Store in an airtight container at room temperature for up to 5 days or in the freezer for up to a month.

Cinnamon Raisin Soft Pretzels

MAKES 10 PRETZELS

That distinctly tangy, somewhat salty, dark brown exterior of a pretzel is just as important as the chewy bread beneath it. To achieve this effect, pretzel makers dip shaped and proofed dough in a lye solution, a strong alkaline that helps the sugars and proteins in the dough turn deep brown in the oven. Lye is also extremely caustic. It can actually dissolve glass! Yikes.

I wanted that characteristic color and flavor on my pretzels, so I initially decided to go for it. You can really buy anything on the Internet these days, and my local hardware store sells classy rubber gloves and protective eyewear. But, alas, I'm a mother now. There is nothing like a downy soft, wide-eyed baby padding around at your feet in the kitchen to make you rethink a big pot of bubbling lye.

Happily, there is a compromise solution. Baking soda is not as strong as lye, but it is much safer for your glassware and loved ones, and produces a similarly tasty effect.

In the bowl of a stand mixer, combine the yeast, water, and 1 tablespoon of the brown sugar. Let it stand until foamy, about 5 minutes. Add the flour, salt, and the remaining brown sugar and mix with the paddle attachment until well combined. Switch to the dough hook and continue to knead until a shaggy dough forms, about 3 minutes. Add the butter pieces, a few at a time, and continue to mix the dough until smooth and pliable, 5 to 7 minutes. Add the raisins and knead to combine. The dough should be supple and smooth and not too sticky. Alternatively, mix together the ingredients in a large bowl, using a wooden spoon. Knead the dough, in the bowl, until it is shaggy, about 3 minutes. Then, knead in the butter pieces until incorporated. Tip out the dough onto a work surface and continue to knead until smooth.

Remove the dough from the bowl, if you haven't already, butter the bowl, and return the dough to the bowl. Cover with plastic wrap and let stand at room temperature until doubled, 1 to 2 hours. Gently expel the air from the dough, knead it into a ball again, cover with plastic wrap, and refrigerate overnight.

Line 2 rimmed baking sheets with silicone baking mats. On a lightly floured surface, cut the dough into 10 equal pieces, about 2½ ounces each. Working with 1 piece a time, roll out to a 16- to 18-inch length. Form into a pretzel shape by first making a U, then twisting the ends around each other and bringing them down to overlap over the bottom. Transfer to the prepared baking sheets and repeat with the remaining dough. Set the shaped pretzels aside to puff for about 25 minutes.

(continued on page 163)

DOUGH:

2¼ teaspoons active dry yeast

¾ cup warm water (110° to 115°F)

¼ cup packed dark brown sugar

3 cups all-purpose flour

2 teaspoons kosher salt

4 tablespoons butter/ ½ stick, cut into pieces, at room temperature, plus more for bowl

2¼ ounces golden raisins (½ cup)

FOR WATER BATH:

⅓ cup baking soda

3 tablespoons dark brown sugar

TO FINISH:

¼ cup granulated sugar

2 teaspoons ground cinnamon

2 tablespoons unsalted butter, melted

Preheat the oven to 425°F.

Prepare the water bath: Bring 8 cups of water to a simmer in a large pot. (Make sure the water is at least a few inches below the rim of the pan, as it will bubble furiously when you add the baking soda.) Add the baking soda and the brown sugar to the water and whisk to combine. Once the bubbles have mostly subsided, carefully add 2 or 3 pretzels to the pot. (I think it's easiest to put the pretzel into the bowl of a spider or large slotted spoon and lower it into the water.) Cook for about 30 seconds to 1 minute per side, then use the spider or slotted spoon to transfer them to the prepared baking sheet. Repeat with the remaining pretzels and set aside.

Bake the first batch of pretzels until puffed and deep golden brown, 15 to 18 minutes. In a small bowl, whisk together the granulated sugar and cinnamon. Brush the warm pretzels with the butter and dip in the cinnamon sugar to coat. Repeat with the remaining pretzels. Serve warm or at room temperature.

Coconut Custard Hand Pies

MAKES 16 HAND PIES

During my pregnancy I liked to read myself a special bedtime story, the "your body this month" section in *What to Expect When You're Expecting*. By my seventh month of pregnancy, the list had swelled (pun intended) to two pages and included some doozies, such as constipation, heartburn, indigestion, flatulence, bloating, headaches, lightheadedness, nosebleeds, sensitive gums, leg cramps, swelling of the ankles and feet, hemorrhoids, varicose veins, stretch marks, shortness of breath, difficulty sleeping, and clumsiness. And I have to give special mention to my absolute favorite: occasional and sudden sharp or shocklike sensations in the pelvic area (a.k.a. "lightning crotch"). Heidi Murkoff, couldn't you have included one positive thing? I mean my hair was truly incredible.

It would have been wise to ignore this section completely. Wondering if and when lightning crotch might strike was not at all helpful. Mamas-to-be, don't read that stuff.

These coconut custard pies are for all the pregnant ladies out there. You deserve a creamy, sweet treat that requires nothing more than one hand to eat. There's a tiny bit of rum to help you pretend it's the cocktail you wish you were drinking. Please put up those swollen legs, grab a good book, and let your growing belly catch flakes of pastry as they fall.

PASTRY:

2¼ cups all-purpose flour, plus more for dusting

¾ teaspoon kosher salt

1¼ cups/2½ sticks cold unsalted butter, cut into pieces

6 to 8 tablespoons ice water

CUSTARD:

4 large egg yolks

½ cup packed light brown sugar

⅓ cup cornstarch

2 cups whole milk

½ cup full-fat coconut milk

1 teaspoon pure vanilla extract

Prepare the pastry: In a food processor, combine the flour, salt, and butter. Pulse until the butter is evenly broken down into ¼-inch pieces. Add the ice water and pulse just until the dough comes together. (Alternatively, you can freeze the butter and then grate it into the flour mixture by hand. Then, use a fork to stir in the water.)

Tip the dough out onto a lightly floured surface. Using a lightly floured rolling pin, roll out the dough to about a 13 x 8-inch rectangle with a short side facing you. Use a bench scraper to help you lift the bottom third up over the middle third and the top third down. This is 1 turn of the dough. Rotate the dough so the seam is to the right side. Repeat that entire process 3 more times, flouring the work surface as necessary. Wrap the dough in plastic wrap and refrigerate for at least 2 hours or up to 2 days. (At this point, you could freeze the dough, well wrapped, for up to 1 month.)

Make the custard: Set a fine-mesh sieve over an 8-inch square baking pan. In a medium saucepan, whisk together the egg yolks and sugar until smooth and creamy. Whisk in the cornstarch. Slowly whisk in the milk, coconut milk, and vanilla until completely smooth. Cook the mixture over

1 cup sweetened shredded coconut, toasted

2 tablespoons unsalted butter

TO ASSEMBLE:

1 large egg, lightly beaten

GLAZE:

½ cup packed light brown sugar

¼ cup heavy cream

4 tablespoons/½ stick unsalted butter

2 teaspoons Lyle's Golden Syrup

¼ teaspoon kosher salt

1 to 2 teaspoons dark rum

medium heat, stirring constantly with a wooden spoon, until it thickens and comes to a very low boil, about 5 minutes. You may have to switch between a whisk and a wooden spoon to keep the custard smooth as you cook it. Continue to cook the custard for 1 minute more. Immediately pour the custard through the sieve. Stir in the shredded coconut and butter. Cover with plastic wrap or waxed paper, making sure to press the plastic into the surface of the custard, and chill completely. At least 30 minutes before you plan to assemble the pies, transfer the custard to the freezer.

Divide the dough in half. Working with 1 piece at a time, on a lightly floured surface, roll the dough out to a 15-inch-diameter circle. Using a 5-inch round cutter, cut 8 circles, transfer to a rimmed baking sheet, cover with plastic wrap, and chill for 30 minutes. Repeat with the remaining dough. If the dough has gotten too soft at this point, pop it back into the fridge to chill.

Preheat the oven to 400°F. Line 2 rimmed baking sheets with parchment paper. Remove the custard from the freezer and divide it into 16 portions. Take 1 dough circle in the palm of your hand, and brush a ½-inch border of beaten egg around the edge. Use an offset spatula to set 1 piece of custard in the center of the circle, and fold the dough over the filling, pinching the edges to seal. Transfer to a prepared baking sheet. Repeat this process with the remaining dough and custard. When all are assembled, use a fork to pinch the edges again and use a sharp paring knife to cut a small slit in the top of each pie. Brush the pies with the beaten egg and bake until puffed and golden brown, 20 to 24 minutes, rotating the sheets halfway through baking. Transfer the pies to a wire rack to cool.

Meanwhile, make the glaze: In a small saucepan, combine the brown sugar, cream, butter, golden syrup, and salt. Cook over medium heat, stirring occasionally, until thick and bubbly, about 6 minutes. Add the rum and cook for another minute. Remove from the heat and let cool and thicken slightly. Drizzle the cooled glaze over the pies to serve.

Double Chocolate Rye Blackout Cookies

MAKES ABOUT 2 DOZEN COOKIES

We couldn't have been more than five or six years old. My friend and I were playing with her dolls in the living room of her house. Apropos of nothing, she stopped playing and looked at me. "My mom said that I shouldn't marry someone that looks like you because if I do, our kids will look like you, too." She had long, pretty blond hair and fair skin. My black hair, cut into a tidy bowl, framed my cocoa-colored face. I wasn't quite sure what she meant, but I knew that her comment didn't make me feel good. I didn't have a response. I nodded in agreement and carried on with the dolls. I wanted the moment to pass, but I didn't want to go home. I didn't want the playing to end. I let her hateful words recede into the darkness of her big house because I didn't understand the larger picture. Neither did she, I assume.

I didn't know what to say then. But I know what to say now. I've made you these superdecadent, bittersweet Double Chocolate Rye Blackout Cookies, adapted from Dorie Greenspan's aptly named World Peace Cookies, because sweetness beats hate. It turns out that brown is beautiful, and delicious, too.

¾ cup all-purpose flour

¾ cup rye flour

⅓ cup cocoa powder, Dutch-processed or natural

¾ teaspoon kosher salt

½ teaspoon baking soda

¾ cup/1½ sticks unsalted butter, at room temperature

¾ cup packed dark brown sugar

1 tablespoon pure vanilla extract

6¾ ounces bittersweet chocolate, finely chopped (about 1½ cups)

In a medium bowl, whisk together the all-purpose flour, rye flour, cocoa powder, salt, and baking soda. In a large bowl, with an electric mixer on medium speed, beat the butter and brown sugar until creamy, about 2 minutes. Add the vanilla and beat to incorporate, scraping down the bowl as necessary. Add the flour mixture and beat until smooth. Then, beat in the chocolate.

Tip out the dough onto a work surface and roll it into a neat cylinder. Transfer the log to a sheet of parchment paper about 18 x 13 inches. Fold the parchment over the dough. Place the long side of a ruler against the bottom edge of the log, on top of the parchment. While pressing firmly on the ruler, pull the top layer of the parchment toward you until you have a smooth 2¼-inch cylinder. Twist the ends to seal. Refrigerate the log for at least 2 hours.

Preheat the oven to 325°F. Line 2 baking sheets with parchment paper. Cut scant ½-inch thick slices from the cold dough, rotating it often to maintain the round shape. Place the slices, about 2 inches apart, on the prepared sheets and bake, 1 sheet at a time, until the cookies look set and dry, 10 to 12 minutes. Transfer the baking sheet to a wire rack to cool until the cookies have hardened, about 5 minutes, then transfer them to the rack to cool completely. Repeat with the remaining slices.

Store the cookies in an airtight container at room temperature for up to 3 days or in the freezer for up to 1 month.

Lemon Lime Earl Grey Sablés

Quick Energy Pickups. That's the first recipe I ever followed. We made them in home economics class. I must have been eight years old. Sweetened peanut butter, confectioners' sugar, and chocolate chips, stirred together, formed into apricot-size balls, and rolled in graham cracker crumbs and sweetened coconut. "Quick energy" is a euphemism for whatever happened to me and my fellow third graders next. I pity the poor math teacher.

These butter cookies are infused with tea leaves, for a buzz that's slightly less chaotic. Earl Grey with its bergamot edge settles in nicely with the zest of lemons and limes.

This recipe is generous, but these little buttons freeze beautifully, should you have leftovers.

In a large bowl, with an electric mixer on medium speed, beat the butter and sugar until combined and fluffy, about 3 minutes. Add the egg yolks, lemon zest, and lime zest and beat until combined. Reduce the speed to low and beat in the flour, tea, baking powder, and salt just until combined.

Divide the dough in half. Tip each half onto a sheet of plastic wrap and shape into a 1¾-inch square log. Freeze the logs until solid, at least 4 hours.

Preheat the oven to 350°F. Line 2 rimmed baking sheets with parchment. Using a sharp knife, cut ¼-inch thick slices from 1 frozen dough log. Place the slices on the prepared baking sheets and bake until set and light golden around the edges, about 15 minutes, rotating the sheets halfway through baking. Transfer the cookies to a wire rack and let cool completely. Repeat with the remaining dough.

Keep the cookies in an airtight container at room temperature for 3 days or in the freezer for up to 2 months.

1 cup/2 sticks unsalted butter, at room temperature

¾ cup granulated sugar

3 large egg yolks

1 teaspoon finely grated lemon zest (from 1 lemon)

1 teaspoon finely grated lime zest (from 1 lime)

2½ cups all-purpose flour

2 tablespoons loose Earl Grey tea

½ teaspoons baking powder

½ teaspoon kosher salt

Profiterole Sundaes

SERVES 4 TO 6

I recently heard that a study found singing to a child has a soothing effect not only on the baby, but also on the singer. When I first lay my son in his crib, he gives me a pleading look. "Don't leave me!" My heart quickens. "I don't want to leave you!" But then I place one hand on his chest, look him in the eyes, and sing:

Savez-vous planter les choux
À la mode, à la mode?
Savez-vous planter les choux
À la mode de chez nous?

I learned the French nursery rhyme when I was small and it stuck. Artie likes it, too. After a few rounds, we both chill out, I tell him that I love him, and I leave. The song may refer to cabbage, but I like to think it's really about choux pastry, which sounds and looks like cabbage. I hope my boy sleeps with visions of sweet puffs dancing in his head.

You can also use these puffs to make either the Cannoli Cream Puffs (page 94), the Pistachio Praline Puffs (page 75), or keep it simple and make profiterole sundaes with store-bought ice cream. Oozy sauces, softly whipped fresh cream, and salty nuts make the whole mess dream-worthy. Take care to bake these puffs really well so that they are crisp. Nobody likes a soggy puff.

PÂTE À CHOUX:

4 tablespoons/½ stick unsalted butter

2 teaspoons granulated sugar

½ teaspoon salt

½ cup all-purpose flour

2 large eggs

CHOCOLATE SAUCE:

½ cup heavy cream

¾ teaspoon instant espresso powder

½ teaspoon kosher salt

4½ ounces bittersweet chocolate, coarsely chopped (1 cup)

Prepare the pâte à choux: Preheat the oven to 400°F. Line 2 rimmed baking sheet with parchment paper.

In a small saucepan, bring ½ cup of water and the butter, sugar, and salt to a simmer over medium heat. As soon as it comes to a simmer, add the flour, stirring constantly until the dough forms a ball and pulls away from the sides of the pan, about 1 minute. Remove the pan from the heat and let the mixture cool for about 3 minutes, stirring the dough occasionally.

Add the eggs, 1 at a time, stirring vigorously between each addition with a wooden spoon. (You can also do this step with an electric mixer.) Drop the dough in 2-tablespoon scoops, about 3 inches apart, on the prepared baking sheets. Bake until deep golden brown and puffed, 22 to 26 minutes, rotating the sheets halfway through baking. Transfer the puffs to a wire rack and let cool completely.

Prepare the chocolate sauce: In a small saucepan, bring the cream, espresso powder, and salt to a simmer over medium heat. Remove from the

CARAMEL SAUCE:

½ cup granulated sugar

½ cup heavy cream

2 tablespoons unsalted butter

1 teaspoon pure vanilla extract

½ teaspoon kosher salt

TO FINISH:

1 pint of your favorite ice cream

Whipped cream

Roasted, salted peanuts

heat and stir in the chocolate. Let the mixture stand for 1 minute, then whisk until smooth.

Prepare the caramel sauce: Place 2 tablespoons of water in a medium saucepan. Add the sugar to the center of the saucepan, making sure the sugar is evenly moistened. Cook over medium heat, without stirring (although you can gently swirl the pan, if necessary) until the caramel is medium amber in color, 5 to 6 minutes. Slowly add the cream, whisking constantly; be careful as it will steam and sputter. Add the butter and cook, whisking constantly, until the caramel is smooth and slightly thickened, about 2 minutes more. Whisk in the vanilla and salt.

To serve, split each puff in half and fill with ice cream. Top with the sauces, cream, and nuts and serve immediately.

French Apple and Fig Tart

SERVE 8 TO 10

I was on my own in Paris, and I had spent the afternoon walking in Montmartre, dodging selfie sticks, looking for a bakery called Les Petits Mitrons. When I got there, I had every good intention of buying just one reasonable slice of its immaculate fruit tart. But then I noticed the other customers. They all looked so content. I imagined that they had parties to get to, families at home waiting for treats, lovers to bestow gifts upon. Each one mirrored my loneliness back at me. I assumed I was the only person eating tarts alone, and I couldn't bear the humiliation. *"Je voudrais toute une tarte, s'il vous plaît,"* I stammered in choppy French. A 10-inch sugar-glazed shield against sadness.

When I got home, I lay my tart on a cutting board and brought it out to the little balcony off the second-floor apartment I was renting. No party. No friends. Just me and my tart. For a minute, I let the self-pity wash over me. I had no one to share it with. Then, I realized: I have no one to share this with! I sliced haphazardly at the edge and carved off a sloppy trapezoid, which I ate with my hands. I cut another piece from the other side and gobbled it down. The edges were crisp and chewy. The fruit dissolved in my mouth and slid down my throat.

I left the tart. I came back to it. I ate tart for dinner. The next day, I wore my new Parisian bathrobe until two p.m. and sliced off pieces of tart whenever I walked by. Sometimes lonely is lucky.

PASTRY:

1½ cups all-purpose flour, plus more for dusting

3 tablespoons granulated sugar

½ teaspoon salt

¾ cup/1½ sticks cold unsalted butter, cut into pieces

5 to 6 tablespoons ice water

TOPPING:

¼ cup granulated sugar, divided

¼ teaspoon cardamom seeds

2 small, crisp apples (about 9 ounces total), peeled, cored, halved, and very thinly sliced (I like Pink Lady, Winesap, or Cortland)

Prepare the pastry: Whisk together the flour, sugar, and salt in a large bowl. Cut in the butter with a pastry blender or 2 knives until the mixture resembles even, coarse sand. Alternatively, pulse the mixture in a food processor until it resembles coarse meal with some slightly large pieces. Add 4 tablespoons of the ice water to the mixture and stir with a fork (or pulse in the processor) until a shaggy dough forms. Add up to 2 more tablespoons of water but stop before the dough gets too wet. It should just hold together when squeezed.

Gather the dough into a rough ball with your hands. Put a piece of plastic wrap on the counter and place the dough on it. Wrap the dough and flatten it into a 6-inch square. Refrigerate until cold, about 2 hours or up to 2 days. Alternatively, freeze the dough, well wrapped, for up to 1 month.

Preheat the oven to 400°F. On a lightly floured, large piece of parchment paper, using a lightly floured rolling pin, roll out the dough to a ¼-inch-thick square (about 12 inches square). Transfer the dough, on its parchment, to a rimmed baking sheet. Freeze for 10 minutes.

Prepare the topping: In a clean spice blender or coffee grinder, process 2 tablespoons of the sugar with the cardamom seeds and transfer to a large bowl. Without breaking the slices, toss the apple slices in the cardamom sugar. Overlap and alternate the apple slices and fig slices in neat rows on

10 Black Mission figs (about 8 ounces), stemmed and thinly sliced crosswise

3 tablespoons unsalted butter, cut into pieces

¼ cup apricot jam, warmed and strained

top of the pastry, leaving a ¼-inch bare border on all 4 sides. Sprinkle evenly with any remaining cardamom sugar and the remaining 2 tablespoons of sugar and dot with the butter pieces. Bake until the crust is deep golden brown and the fruit is tender, 40 to 45 minutes. Immediately after pulling the tart from the oven, run a flat spatula around the edges to loosen it from any caramelized sugar on the pan.

Brush the warm tart with the strained apricot jam. Serve warm or at room temperature.

Maple Cream Pie

SERVES 8 TO 10

Next time I notice the laugh lines that bracket my smile, I'm going to think of maple syrup. The American treasure should be rebranded a cheery symbol for aging. Maple syrup starts as sap from a sugar maple tree. It's clear and thin. Fresh faced and fast moving. But youth is not the prime of its life. When it's new and light, the sap has little complexity. Maple syrup only become sweet and luscious, bold and wise once it has spent time boiling. It has to brown, thicken, and slow to become truly wonderful.

Keep a close eye on this crust during the blind bake. The walnuts can push the crust from perfectly golden to unpleasantly dark in the blink of an eye. The cloud of whipped cream should not be sweetened. Not only does whipped cream have an excellent natural dairy flavor that can be muted by too much sugar, the pie itself is sweet enough.

Prepare the pastry: In a food processor, combine the walnuts and sugar and pulse until the nuts are finely ground. Add the flour and salt and pulse to incorporate. Add the butter and pulse until the mixture is the texture of coarse meal with some pea-size pieces. Add 2 tablespoons of the ice water and pulse until the dough is evenly moistened. The dough should hold together when squeezed, but not be too wet. Add up to 2 more tablespoons of ice water, if necessary. Tip out the dough onto a piece of plastic wrap and using the plastic to gather the dough together, form it into a disk. Chill for at least 2 hours or up to 2 days. (Alternatively, you can freeze the dough for up to 1 week.)

Preheat the oven to 375°F. On a lightly floured surface, roll out the dough into a 12-inch-diameter round (about ⅛ inch thick). Transfer the dough to a 9-inch standard pie plate. Trim the excess dough and fold it to make a decorative edge. Wrap in plastic wrap and freeze for at least 15 minutes.

Line the frozen shell with parchment paper or foil and fill with pie weights. Bake the crust until the edges are lightly golden and the crust beneath the parchment is dry, about 25 minutes. Remove the parchment and weights and continue to bake the crust until it is golden brown, 15 to 20 minutes. Transfer the pan to a wire rack to cool completely. Set a fine-mesh sieve next to the crust for later.

Prepare the filling: In a small saucepan, bring the maple syrup to a boil over high heat, then lower the heat to maintain a gentle simmer. Continue to cook the syrup until it has reduced by about half, about 12 minutes.

(continued on next page)

PASTRY:

1½ ounces walnuts (about ⅓ cup)

1 tablespoon granulated sugar

1½ cups all-purpose flour, plus more for dusting

½ teaspoon kosher salt

½ cup/1 stick cold unsalted butter, cut into pieces

2 to 4 tablespoons ice water

FILLING:

1¼ cups pure maple syrup

6 large egg yolks

¼ cup cornstarch

2 cups whole milk

1 cup heavy cream

½ teaspoon kosher salt

2 tablespoons unsalted butter

TO FINISH:

1 cup cold heavy cream, whipped to soft peaks

(You can occasionally pour the syrup into a glass measuring cup to check the volume.)

In a medium saucepan (away from the stovetop), whisk the egg yolks with the cornstarch until smooth. In a slow stream, while whisking, add the milk and cream. Add the salt, butter, and reduced maple syrup. Don't worry if the syrup seizes. It will smooth out in the next step when you heat the custard.

Cook the milk mixture over medium heat, stirring constantly with a wooden spoon, until it has thickened and come to a very low boil, about 7 minutes. Cook the custard for 1 minute more and then pour it through the sieve into the cooled crust and spread it out evenly. Press a piece of waxed paper directly onto the surface of the custard and transfer the pie to the fridge. Chill the pie for at least 4 hours or up to overnight. To serve, top the pie with whipped cream.

Old-Fashioned Old-Fashioned Doughnuts

MAKES ABOUT 10 DOUGHNUTS

When I first called my parents with the news that I was pregnant, my mom screamed, just like in the movies. She confessed that she had a feeling (she often gets "a feeling" based on pretty much nothing). I could hear the smile in my dad's voice as he asked me general questions about my health and the obstetrician I had chosen. Then, he got serious. "You know, you're really going to have to be careful with your drinking now." I laughed so hard I spit all over the phone. First of all, Dad, I know that. And second, I don't drink that much! I gave a famously bad presentation at a brewery once about dessert and beer pairings that led off with the fact that I don't drink beer or really even enjoy it. Two glasses of wine is my sweet spot. I'm excited about a Manhattan or an old-fashioned on a special occasion, but I'd be equally happy with one of those beautiful ice cubes floating in a glass of ginger ale. So, I promised my dad I would try. Don't worry, Grandpa. I was plenty happy to stick to doughnuts instead.

Prepare the dough: In a medium bowl, whisk together the all-purpose flour, rye flour, baking powder, salt, nutmeg, and baking soda. In a large bowl, beat the butter, granulated sugar, and orange zest until creamy, about 2 minutes. Add the egg to the butter mixture and beat to combine. Alternate adding the flour mixture and the buttermilk and orange juice to the butter mixture, starting and ending with the flour mixture. Transfer the dough to a piece of plastic warp, wrap it well, and refrigerate for at least 1 hour or up to overnight. The dough will be sticky.

On a floured surface, roll out the dough to ½ inch thick. Use a 3-inch round cookie cutter to cut 10 circles from the dough. Use a 1½-inch round cutter to cut the center out of each circle. (You can fry the holes, too!) You can reroll the scraps once and cut out about 2 more doughnuts. Liberally dust a parchment-lined baking sheet with flour. Transfer the cut doughnuts to the prepared sheet, cover, and chill until firm, about 20 minutes.

Clip a candy thermometer to a heavy-bottomed pot and heat the oil to 350°F. Meanwhile, line a rimmed baking sheet with a few layers of paper towels. Carefully drop 3 or 4 doughnuts and holes into the hot oil. Fry until golden brown and puffed, about 2 minutes per side. (You may have to turn the heat up or down to maintain the temperature.) Using a spider or a slotted spoon, transfer the doughnuts to the prepared baking sheet to drain any excess oil. Let stand for about 2 minutes.

(continued on next page)

DOUGH:

2 cups all-purpose flour, plus more for dusting

1 cup rye flour

2 teaspoons baking powder

1 teaspoon kosher salt

½ teaspoon freshly grated nutmeg

¼ teaspoon baking soda

4 tablespoons/½ stick unsalted butter, at room temperature

¾ cup granulated sugar

2 tablespoons finely grated orange zest (from 1 orange)

1 large egg

½ cup buttermilk, at room temperature

¼ cup freshly squeezed orange juice

1½ quarts (6 cups) vegetable oil for frying

ORANGE SUGAR:

½ cup granulated sugar

1 teaspoon finely grated orange zest

GLAZE:

1 cup confectioners' sugar

1 to 2 tablespoons freshly squeezed orange juice

1 tablespoon whiskey (optional)

Prepare the orange sugar: In a medium bowl, toss the granulated sugar with the orange zest.

Prepare the glaze: In another medium bowl, whisk together the confectioners' sugar, orange juice, and whiskey (if using). Toss 5 of the warm doughnuts in the orange sugar. Dip the other 5 in the glaze. Serve immediately.

Orange Pistachio Buns

MAKES 12 BUNS

I found a sensible skirt and creamy white sweater, put on some lipstick, and left the baby with his dad. I was off to meet the co-op board for the apartment I was hoping to buy. Its approval was my last hurdle to clear. The board members grilled me about my income and the terms of my divorce. They asked me to let the entire building know if I planned to have houseguests. They made sure I understood the rug policy. I answered their questions dutifully, thinking all the while that I should have just brought them buns, to save us the trouble of playing Forty Questions. Food can say so much more than words. One bite and any concerns about my joining their building would have just melted away.

This is the recipe I want to play me in the movie of my life. First of all, these buns are lovely to look at, each a vibrant swirl of pistachio and orange. At the same time, they're also fragrant and sweet, with just the right ratio of crunchy exterior to tender, buttery middle. And finally, they're savvy and capable, shining as breakfast, snack, or dessert.

If you want squidgier buns, use a 9-inch round cake pan and cut the buns into 9 pieces instead of 12. And if you'd like a little extra flair, mix together a simple glaze with some confectioners' sugar, milk, and orange zest.

Prepare the dough: Heat the milk in a small pot over medium heat. (Watch closely. Milk loves to boil over!) Transfer to the bowl of a stand mixer fitted with the dough hook and let cool to 110° to 115°F. It should be warm to the touch. Add the yeast and 1 teaspoon of the sugar and let stand until foamy, about 5 minutes.

Add the remaining sugar, egg, and egg yolk. With the mixer on low speed, add the flour, then the salt. Knead on medium-low speed, for about 5 minutes. The dough should come together into a neat ball without sticking to the sides of the bowl.

With the mixer running, add the butter, a few pieces at a time. Depending on the size of your mixer bowl, you may have to stop the mixer and knead the butter in a bit before the mixer can really grip the dough and do its job. Knead the dough until it is smooth and elastic, about 8 minutes. Remove the bowl from the mixer, cover it with plastic wrap, and leave it in a warm place to double. Alternatively, mix together the ingredients in a large bowl, using a wooden spoon. Knead the dough, in the bowl, until it is shaggy, about 3 minutes. Then, knead in the butter pieces until incorporated. Tip out the dough onto a work surface and continue to knead until smooth. (continued on next page)

DOUGH:

⅔ cup whole milk

¼ cup plus 1 teaspoon granulated sugar

2¼ teaspoons active dry yeast

1 large egg, lightly beaten

1 large egg yolk, lightly beaten

2½ cups all-purpose flour

½ teaspoon kosher salt

6 tablespoons/¾ stick unsalted butter, at room temperature, plus more for pan

FILLING:

3 ounces unsalted, raw pistachios (about ¾ cup)

⅓ cup granulated sugar

4 tablespoons/ ½ stick unsalted butter, softened

3 tablespoons finely grated orange zest (from 3 oranges)

½ teaspoon kosher salt

TO FINISH:

4 tablespoons/½ stick unsalted butter, melted

Granulated sugar for rolling

Meanwhile, prepare the filling: In a food processor, pulse the pistachios and sugar until finely ground (but not paste) and transfer to a bowl. In another bowl combine the butter, orange zest, and salt.

Turn out the dough onto a work surface. (You shouldn't need flour at this point.) Roll the dough into a 16 x 12-inch rectangle. The dough should feel like heaven in your hands, soft and supple, and it should be easy to work with. Spread orange butter mixture evenly over the surface and then sprinkle evenly with the nut mixture. Gently press the nut mixture into the butter to adhere. Starting at the long end, tightly roll up the dough and pinch the seam closed. Generously butter a standard 12-well muffin tin. Cut the roll crosswise into 12 equal pieces. Transfer to the prepared pan, cut-side down, cover with plastic wrap, and let rest until dough is puffed to fill the cups and about ⅛ inch above the rims.

Preheat the oven to 350°F. Uncover the buns and bake until golden brown, 18 to 22 minutes. Transfer the tin to a wire rack to cool for 5 minutes. Using an offset spatula, remove the buns from the tin and transfer to the rack.

Brush the buns with the melted butter and dip them in the sugar. Serve warm or at room temperature.

Glazed Chocolate Doughnut Waffles

MAKES 4 BELGIAN WAFFLES

I've never actually seen the movie *Frozen*, but my nieces taught me the song "Let It Go," and it has gotten me through some tough moments. The rage I felt looking at that guy on the subway who was playing video games audibly and leaning on the pole so that no one else could hold on? Let it go! That time I had one too many glasses of wine at a wedding and said something stupid to the *New York Times* reporter who was covering the event for the Vows section? Let it go! The fact that somebody who shall remain nameless fed the baby raspberry jam in his yogurt when I had expressly ruled "no sugar before one"? Let it go!

Glazed chocolate cake doughnuts are my absolute favorite. I love the sugary crackle that gives way to crisp fried edges and that squidgy, cakey center. But I just can't get them right from scratch. And believe me have I tried. Dozens of times. No matter what I do, the final product falls flat. Scorched. Dry. Sad. So, guess what I did? I let it go and came up with something that I think might even be better. These waffles cook up quickly, with crunchy edges and soft middles. Serve them whole for a decadent brunch, with a couple scoops of ice cream for dessert, or broken into quarters as cookies.

Set a wire rack inside a rimmed baking sheet.

Prepare the waffle batter: In a large bowl, whisk together the flour, cocoa powder, brown sugar, yeast, baking powder, and salt. In a medium bowl, whisk together the eggs, milk, butter, and vanilla. Fold the wet ingredients into the dry ingredients. Fold in the chocolate. Let the batter rest at room temperature for 30 minutes.

Prepare the glaze: Melt the butter in a small saucepan. Add the confectioner's sugar, cocoa powder, milk, and salt and whisk until thick and smooth. Pour the glaze into a pie plate and cover with plastic wrap.

Heat your waffle iron according to the manufacturer's instructions. Butter the iron and pour in 1 cup of batter, close the iron, and cook until waffle is crisp, about 8 minutes. Transfer the cooked waffle to the wire rack to cool. Repeat with the remaining batter.

Dip 1 side of each waffle into the glaze and set back on the rack, glaze-side up, to set slightly. Serve immediately.

WAFFLES:

2 cups all-purpose flour

½ cup Dutch-processed cocoa powder

⅓ cup packed brown sugar

1½ teaspoons active dry yeast

1½ teaspoons baking powder

¾ teaspoon kosher salt

2 large eggs

1¾ cups warm milk

6 tablespoons/¾ stick unsalted butter, melted, plus more for waffle iron

2 teaspoons pure vanilla extract

2¼ ounces bittersweet chocolate, finely chopped (about ½ cup)

GLAZE:

2 tablespoons unsalted butter

2 cups confectioners' sugar

1 tablespoon cocoa powder

4–5 tablespoons whole milk

Big pinch of kosher salt

Peach and Raspberry Almond Pie

SERVES 8 TO 10

A few years ago, I was driving through rural North Carolina and starving. Instead of pulling over at a fried chicken chain, I ate nuts. Cashews and peanuts go down easy at first. They're fatty and salty and hit the spot. Until they don't, and they become the spot. Thirty minutes into gorging on nuts you've got what I now call "nut gut." That's the feeling of being stuffed with nuts but still strangely hungry. It's empty satiety. If only those nuts were baked into a southern peach pie. Then, I'd really have been full.

I prefer baking fruit pies into galettes or in shallow tart pans. In a standard pie plate, the ratio of fruit to crust just isn't right. I want every bite of pie to have equal parts jammy, slumpy-sweet cooked fruit and salty, buttery pastry. I think I wouldn't even mind a little more of the latter.

Prepare the pastry: In a food processor, combine the almonds and granulated sugar and pulse until finely ground. Add the flour and salt and pulse to incorporate. Add the butter and pulse until the mixture is the texture of coarse meal with some pea-size pieces. Add 4 tablespoons of the ice water and pulse until the dough is evenly moistened. The dough should hold together when squeezed but not be too wet. Add up to 2 more tablespoons of ice water, if necessary. Divide the dough in half, wrap each portion in plastic wrap, and form 2 disks. Chill for at least 1 hour or up to 2 days. (Alternatively, you can freeze the dough for up to 1 week.)

Preheat the oven to 400°F.

Meanwhile, on a lightly floured surface, roll out 1 disk of dough to a ⅛-inch-thick circle, about 10 inches in diameter. Fit the disk into the bottom and sides of a 9-inch fluted tart pan with a removable bottom and trim the excess. Wrap well and chill for at least 30 minutes. On a piece of parchment paper, roll out the other disk to a 12-inch circle and cut it into 1-inch strips. Transfer the strips on their parchment to a baking sheet, cover with plastic wrap, and chill until ready to use.

Prepare the filling: In a large bowl, gently toss together the peaches, raspberries, brown sugar, cornstarch, almond extract, and salt. Transfer the mixture to the dough-lined tart pan and dot with the butter. To create a lattice with the remaining pastry, first top the pie evenly with 5 of the pastry strips laid on top in parallel. Think of the strips as numbered 1 to 5. Fold strips 2 and 4 halfway over themselves and lay another pastry strip (6) in the opposite direction on top of the pie. Unfold strips 2 and 4 over 6. Then, fold back strips 1, 3, and 5 back and slip another strip (7) over the top of the pie. Fold strips 1, 3, and 5 back overs strip 7. Continue with this pattern until (continued on next page)

PASTRY:

3 ounces sliced almonds (¾ cup)

3 tablespoons granulated sugar

1¾ cups all-purpose flour, plus more for dusting

1 teaspoon kosher salt

14 tablespoons/1¾ sticks cold, unsalted butter

4 to 6 tablespoons ice water

FILLING:

2 pounds peaches, peeled, pitted, and sliced in ¼-inch wedges

6 ounces fresh raspberries (1 cup)

½ cup packed light brown sugar

3 tablespoons cornstarch

¼ teaspoon almond extract

Pinch of kosher salt

1 tablespoon unsalted butter, cut into pieces

TO FINISH:

1 large egg, beaten

Sanding sugar for sprinkling (optional)

you've used all of the strips evenly over the top. Press the excess dough off the edge all the way around.

Brush the pastry with the beaten egg and sprinkle with sanding sugar (if using). Place the tart pan on a parchment-lined rimmed baking sheet and bake until the pastry is deep golden brown and the filling is bubbling even in the center. Transfer the tart pan to a rack to cool for at least 2 hours. Serve warm or room temperature. This pie is best served slightly warm or at room temperature. Leftovers might not be perfect but make a tasty breakfast nonetheless.

Roasted White Chocolate, Almond, Oat Cookies

MAKES ABOUT 2 DOZEN COOKIES

Parenting rules used to be a little more relaxed in the early 1980s. Whenever my mom and I would go to the supermarket, I would wander. As soon as I got out of sight, I always made a beeline for the bakery counter, where I paced back and forth in front of the case, inspecting the mounds of cookies piled high. Neon pink and green leaves sandwiched with chocolate and jam. Technicolor rainbow cookies. Big, dense double chocolate cookies. And my favorite, oatmeal cookies studded with nuts and chocolate.

Then, I went to work. I made my eyes look as wide as humanly possible and smiled the biggest, toothiest grin I could muster. I lingered just long enough to make the sweet, hair-netted lady behind the case feel sorry for me. Maybe she thought I was lost and hungry. Maybe she just wanted me to go away. She handed me a cookie, wrapped in a small square of bakery paper, which I graciously accepted with a look of surprise and glee, and then skipped off to find my mom. Cookie scam artist.

Try these as is or as the bookends of an ice-cream sandwich. A bitter coffee ice cream or tart raspberry sorbet would be nice. If you generally find yourself in the anti–white chocolate camp, I implore you to roast it. The process takes an hour, but it's easy and deeply satisfying and the final product is toasty and wonderful. Using a spatula to smear chocolate over a warm sheet pan, watching it seize and relax over and over again, rivals any meditation retreat. That said, if you can find Valrhona's Dulcey Blond Chocolate, a beautiful toasted white chocolate, buy it and use that. You will not be sorry.

Preheat the oven to 250°F. Put the chocolate on a rimmed baking sheet and bake for 10 minutes. Remove the baking sheet from the oven and scrape up and stir the chocolate with an offset spatula, then spread it out again. Don't worry if it changes texture a few times from crumbly to smooth. It should smooth out in the end. Bake for 10 minutes and then scrape and spread the chocolate again. Repeat this process about 6 times, until the chocolate is the deep caramel color. Transfer the chocolate to a piece of parchment and let it harden. Chop the chocolate and store it in an airtight container at room temperature until you're ready to make cookies (up to 1 week).

Preheat the oven to 350°F and line 2 rimmed baking sheets with parchment paper.

In a large bowl, with a wooden spoon, mix together the almond butter, butter, brown sugar, and granulated sugar until smooth and creamy. Stir in the egg. Then, add the oats, flour, salt, baking soda, and cinnamon and stir until combined. Stir in the almonds and the chocolate.

(continued on next page)

6 ounces good-quality white chocolate (not chips), chopped (about 1½ cups)

½ cup unsweetened almond butter

6 tablespoons/¾ stick unsalted butter, at room temperature

½ cup packed dark brown sugar

¼ cup granulated sugar

1 large egg, at room temperature

1½ cups old-fashioned rolled oats

¾ cup all-purpose flour

¾ teaspoon kosher salt

½ teaspoon baking soda

½ teaspoon ground cinnamon

4 ounces sliced almonds (1 cup)

Portion the dough into 3-tablespoon scoopfuls. Roll each scoop into a nice ball and place, at least 1 inch apart, on the prepared pans. Bake until the cookies have spread and are just dry in the center, but still a bit soft, 12 to 14 minutes, rotating the pans halfway through baking. Let the cookies cool on the pans for 5 minutes, then transfer them to wire racks to cool completely. Repeat with the remaining dough.

Store the cooled cookies in an airtight container at room temperature for up to 3 days and in the freezer for 3 months.

Rum Raisin Slab Pie

SERVES 10

Here's a life lesson: practically everything tastes good between buttery slabs of pastry. One cold winter night, I was craving pie but had nothing in the way of fresh fruit handy. I rummaged through the pantry and found a big box of raisins. Raisins aren't glamorous. They're not expensive or chic. Institutions feed them to children and old people. When I announced that I was about to make a raisin pie, everyone groaned. But I know the golden pastry rule.

So, I plumped my raisins in plenty of rum and brown sugar, threw in a good shot of lemon, and spread them between two big sheets of pastry, shards of golden butter visible throughout. The resulting pie was sweet but complex, rich, and quite popular among the doubters. In fact, not one person had a complaint. Except when it came to the name. "You can't call this *raisin pie*. It's so much better than that."

Prepare the pastry: In a food processor, combine the flour, granulated sugar, and salt and pulse to mix. Add the butter and pulse until the mixture is the texture of coarse meal with some pea-size pieces. Add 6 tablespoons of ice water and pulse until the dough is evenly moistened. The dough should hold together when squeezed, but not be too wet. Add up to 3 more tablespoons of water, if necessary. Divide the dough in half, wrap each portion in plastic wrap, and form 2 rectangles. Chill for at least 1 hour or up to 2 days. (Alternatively, you can freeze the dough for up to 1 week.)

Meanwhile, prepare the filling: In a medium saucepan, combine the golden raisins, raisins, rum, and 1 cup of water and bring to a boil over medium-high heat. Cook, stirring occasionally, until the raisins are plump and the liquid has reduced by about half, about 6 minutes. Add the brown sugar and continue to cook until the liquid is syrupy, about 4 minutes. Stir in the cornstarch and cook for 1 minute longer. Remove from the heat and stir in the lemon zest and salt. Transfer the raisin mixture to a plate, cover with plastic wrap, and transfer to the fridge to cool.

Preheat the oven to 400°F.

On a lightly floured surface, roll out 1 portion of dough to a 12 x 10-inch rectangle. Transfer to a piece of parchment paper on a work surface. Repeat with the remaining portion of dough.

(continued on page 191)

PASTRY:

2¼ cups all-purpose flour

3 tablespoons granulated sugar

1 teaspoon kosher salt

1 cup/2 sticks cold unsalted butter, cut into pieces

6 to 9 tablespoons ice water

FILLING:

9 ounces golden raisins (2 cups)

4½ ounces raisins (1 cup)

½ cup dark rum

½ cup packed dark brown sugar

1 tablespoon cornstarch

2 tablespoons finely grated lemon zest

½ teaspoon kosher salt

1 tablespoon cold unsalted butter, cut into small pieces

Top 1 dough rectangle with the raisin filling, spreading it out to an even layer and leaving a 1-inch bare border all the way around. Sprinkle the butter evenly over the top.

Brush the beaten egg on all 4 edges. Top with the remaining rectangle of dough. Use a fork to crimp the 4 edges together. Use a sharp knife to trim about ⅛ to ¼ inch off each edge. Use the parchment paper to lift the pie onto a rimmed baking sheet. Cut 4 small slits in the top sheet of dough. Cover and freeze the pie for 15 minutes.

Brush the top of the pie with beaten egg. Bake until deep golden brown and crisp, about 40 minutes. Transfer the pie, on its baking sheet, to a wire rack to cool. Serve warm or at room temperature with ice cream.

This pie is best the day it's made but leftovers can be stored at room temperature for up to 3 days.

TO FINISH:
1 large egg, lightly beaten
Vanilla ice cream for serving

Saffron and Chocolate Tea Cake

SERVES 8

What makes a good love match? Chocolate needs a grown-up playmate. He needs to stop partying with gobs of ice cream, neon cherries, rainbow sprinkles, sugary goo, and just come back to earth. Cheesecake takes advantage of him. Marshmallows are clearly a bad influence.

Saffron is smart and sensible. She's just the bright and slightly acerbic partner that he badly needs. She puts him in his place, gets that sweetness in check, and adds color, depth, and sophistication.

Preheat the oven to 350°F. Butter and flour an 8½ x 4½-inch loaf pan.

In a small saucepan, bring the milk and saffron to a simmer over medium heat. Immediately remove from the heat, cover, and let stand for at least 15 minutes.

In a medium bowl, whisk together the flour, baking powder, and salt.

In a small bowl, whisk together the saffron milk and the yogurt. In a large bowl, with an electric mixer on medium-high speed, beat the butter and granulated sugar together until fluffy, about 3 minutes. Reduce the speed to medium and add the eggs, 1 at a time, then the vanilla. Alternate adding the flour mixture and the milk mixture, beginning and ending with the flour mixture, scraping down the bowl as necessary. Fold in the chocolate.

Transfer the batter to the prepared pan and smooth the top. Sprinkle the top liberally with sanding sugar. Bake until puffed and a toothpick inserted into the center comes out with moist crumbs attached, 60 to 70 minutes. Transfer the pan to a rack and let cool for 15 minutes. Using a sharp knife, carefully loosen the cake from the edges of the pan, tip out the cake, and set it right-side up on the rack to cool completely.

The cake is best the day it's made, but leftovers can be stored in an airtight container at room temperature for up to 3 days or frozen for up to a month.

¾ cup/1½ sticks unsalted butter, at room temperature, plus more for pan

½ cup whole milk

¼ teaspoon saffron threads

2 cups all-purpose flour, plus more for pan

2 teaspoons baking powder

½ teaspoon kosher salt

½ cup whole-milk yogurt, at room temperature

1 cup granulated sugar

3 large eggs, at room temperature

1 teaspoon pure vanilla extract

4½ ounces bittersweet chocolate, chopped (1 cup)

Sanding sugar for sprinkling

Unorthodox Challah with Dates and Cocoa

MAKES 1 LOAF

A perfectly braided challah is a sight to behold. I know because I've seen them in bakeries. Mine are never so. I usually get confused halfway through the folding and start tucking bits of the dough under other bits willy-nilly. If you want precise directions on how to wrap up a neat four-strand loaf, allow me to suggest an online tutorial. Or you could just trust me when I say that it doesn't matter. Just do your best. It's going to look great, it's going to smell like heaven, and it's going to be gone in a minute.

DOUGH:

2¼ teaspoons active dry yeast

⅓ cup plus 1 tablespoon granulated sugar, divided

¾ cup warm water (110° to 115°F)

4 cups all-purpose flour, plus more if necessary

6 tablespoons melted coconut oil, plus more for bowl

2 large eggs, at room temperature

2 large egg yolks, at room temperature

1 teaspoon kosher salt

FILLING:

6 Medjool dates, pitted (½ cup)

¼ cup warm water

2 tablespoons dark brown sugar

2 tablespoons cocoa powder, Dutch-processed or natural

1 tablespoon coconut oil

¼ teaspoon ground cinnamon

Pinch of kosher salt

In the bowl of a stand mixer with the dough hook attached, or a large bowl, combine the yeast, 1 tablespoon of the granulated sugar, and the warm water and let stand until foamy, about 5 minutes. Add the flour, coconut oil, eggs, egg yolks, salt, and remaining ⅓ cup of sugar and knead on medium-low speed (or by hand) until the dough is smooth and elastic, about 10 minutes. This is a sticky dough, so if you're kneading by hand, use a bench scraper in 1 hand while you work to constantly scrape the work surface and your hands. You can add 1 to 2 tablespoons of flour, if necessary, but don't add too much. Scrape down the bowl, coat it with a very light sheen of coconut oil, and add the dough. Cover and set the dough aside to rise until doubled in size. This could take anywhere from 45 minutes to 2 hours. Gently knead the dough a few times to expel the air bubbles and set it aside until it has doubled again.

Meanwhile, make the filling: In a food processor, pulse the dates, warm water, brown sugar, cocoa powder, coconut oil, cinnamon, and salt until smooth, scraping down the bowl occasionally. Transfer the filling to a bowl. Don't leave a drop behind!

Tip out the dough onto a very lightly floured surface and divide it in half. Roll out 1 portion to about a 13 x 9-inch rectangle. Spread half of the filling evenly over the rectangle then, starting from 1 of the long ends, roll it up into a tight coil. Pinch the seam and the ends to seal the coil. Repeat with the other portion of dough.

Now, working with 1 coil at a time, carefully roll and stretch the dough to about a 3-foot length. Cut the length in half and pinch the ends to seal. Repeat with the other coil.

You can shape the 4 strands any way you like. To make a round braided challah, start by laying the strands out like a # sign with the 2 vertical strips on top of the 2 horizontal strips. Starting from the top left corner, let's go around clockwise and call the ends A, B, C, D, E, F, G, and H.

TO FINISH:

1 large egg, lightly beaten

**Pearl sugar for sprinkling
(optional)**

First, put B under C, then F under G. Moving counterclockwise, cross D over C, B over A, F over E, and H over G. You've just taken each end that was under and put it over the strand to its left. Now, moving clockwise, cross C over F and repeat that process, taking the strands that are now under and crossing them over the strand to the right. Repeat this process again, counterclockwise. Once you run out of length, tuck the ends underneath. Transfer the braid to a parchment-lined baking sheet, cover loosely with plastic wrap, and let stand until puffed, 45 minutes to 1½ hours. During the last half hour, preheat the oven to 375°F.

Carefully brush the loaf with 2 coats of beaten egg and sprinkle with pearl sugar (if using). Bake until the loaf is deep golden brown and an instant-read thermometer reads 180° to 190°F when inserted into the center, 40 to 45 minutes. Tent with foil if the bread is browning too quickly. Transfer the challah to a wire rack to cool before slicing.

ACKNOWLEDGMENTS

Growing a cookbook is much like raising a child: it takes a village. I want to extend my warmest thank you to my beloved village.

My agent, Janis Donnaud, was feisty when I needed her to be and kind when it counted. Any author would be lucky to have her and Teresa Cavanaugh on her side. I'm grateful for the cheerleading and the tough love both.

Jenny Abramson, Valerie Bischoff, Erin Chapman, Jill Cohen, Cate Conmy, Paulie Dibner, Deborah Keefe, Amy Leo, Cathy Lo, Jenn Marsidi, Emilie Raffa, Abby Rasminsky, Laura Rege, Sarah Rosenthal, Jason Schreiber, Christo Sedgewick, Nicki Sizemore, Martha Tinkler, Lauryn Tyrell, and Merritt Watts tested the heck out of these recipes. Grace Elkus went above and beyond. These recipes are infinitely better because of all of them.

This book looks as wonderful as it does because of a veritable food photography dream team. Photographer Julia Gartland and her assistant Jessica Pettway worked with me to create these stunning images, over and over again in some cases, until they were just right. Ali Slagle, with her keen scavenger's eye, styled it beautifully, infusing the pages with gorgeous props and also things that she thoughtfully plucked from my home, Marian Bull's home (Thanks, Marian!), and my neighbor's garden. (Shout out to Maja Säfström. Her whimsical drawing of two otters hung in Artie's nursery until Ali decided it would make a perfect image for the opener of Love. And to Paulie, who made Artie's lovely fox friend.) Pearl Jones worked tirelessly in the kitchen and cranked out some of the most gorgeous food I have ever seen. Molly Wenk and Taylor Murray pinch-hit with style.

Many thanks to the exquisite team at Running Press. Kristen Green Wiewora and Amanda Richmond helped me make my silly feelings about cake something worth reading.

Augustine Sedgewick's help on this project, from the seed of the idea to the final edit, was invaluable. Thanks, Joe.

Lina Priscilla Perez Bolanos cared for Artie with such love and kindness while I was holed up in the kitchen and my office. She made it possible for me to focus on this book without worrying about him. You are a part of our family forever and we love you.

To Suneetha and Upali Seneviratne, my dear parents. I don't think I've ever needed you more than I have over these last few years. You've been the source of so much comfort, love, and support. I am so very lucky to have you.

INDEX